ADVANCE PRAISE
To Fool The Rain

All of us at BRAC are so proud of the success of Fonkoze's *Chemen Lavi Miyò* program, which we helped them pilot and begin to scale up. I am confident that anyone truly interested in learning how we can eliminate extreme poverty in this world will want to read *To Fool the Rain* because it focuses on the stories of the participants themselves — the women judged to be among the very poorest in their villages, who undertake the struggle to bring their families out of the kind of poverty that leaves families without hope. It explains so beautifully how the CLM staff work with the families every week for 18 months to help them build the confidence, the livelihoods, the skills and the assets that result in effective futures for them. In Bangladesh, we've seen how the effects of this program last long into the future, and I'm sure the same will occur in Haiti. Families become resilient to future shocks and children grow up to lead successful lives of their own. Generational cycles of poverty are broken. I want to congratulate the staff and the thousands of CLM participants on their successes — and Steven Werlin for capturing not only the dignity of these women, but also the essence of how this program transforms lives.

Sir Fazle Hasan Abed
Founder and Chairperson, BRAC

Steven Werlin's *To Fool the Rain* is an important contribution to the growing body of literature on development efforts in Haiti. Werlin takes us on a riveting journey down narrow dirt paths and up steep ravines to introduce us to some of the courageous women in Haiti's Central Plateau who are climbing a staircase out of extreme poverty through Fonkoze's *Chemen Lavi Miyò* program.

For anyone considering a career in the public sector or civil society, this book is a must read, as Werlin reminds us that the work of human development is ultimately about humans, and that we in government or the international aid community, in order to be more effective, must know and communicate with the people we aim to serve.

Gérald Oriol, Jr.
Haiti's Secretary of State for the
Integration of Persons with Disabilities

For decades, humanitarian leaders have wrung their hands about what can be done to permanently improve the lives of the ultra-poor. Many have concluded that nothing can be done except to wait for economic growth to pick up, even though the poorest people and their children are unlikely to survive to enjoy the trickle-down benefits. Steve Werlin and his colleagues at Fonkoze have boldly rejected such thinking. Through painstaking study of a breakthrough in Bangladesh, and endless experimentation and tinkering to adapt it to rural Haiti, they came up with "Pathway to a Better Life." This intensive, 18-month program has been shown to permanently change the life circumstances of some of the most marginalized and destitute people on the planet. In his book, Werlin tells the story of this achievement in very human terms, drawing on his years of work in the most remote parts of a country often described as a failed state. His deep insights about Haitian society and the culture of poverty come through on every page. *To Fool the Rain* should be required reading for anyone who has either dreamed or doubted that a poverty-free world is achievable, or wondered what it would actually take to realize that ideal.

Alex Counts
Founder, Grameen Foundation

In February 2015, I travelled to my country of birth to see firsthand the work of Fonkoze. For me, the experience was life changing and moved me to increased action. I was most stirred to see the work with Haiti's most vulnerable women and families. We hiked through the mountains with Steven Werlin to meet members of Fonkoze's *Chemen Lavi Miyò*, hear their stories of progress, and see the courage in their eyes. In *To Fool the Rain*, Steven is able to capture so eloquently and respectfully, the day-to-day lives and struggles of these brave women. It is a prayer lifted on their behalf.

Garcelle Beauvais
Actress, author, and talk show host

To Fool the Rain

To Fool the • Rain

Haiti's Poor and Their Pathway to a Better Life

By

STEVEN WERLIN

TI KOZE PRESS

FIRST TI KOZE PRESS EDITION

Published in the United States by Ti Koze Press
1718 Connecticut Ave NW, Suite 201, Washington, DC 20009

ISBN 9-7809973633-0-2 (hardcover)
ISBN 978-0-9973633-1-9 (paperback)
ISBN 978-0-9973633-2-6 (ebook)

LIBRARY OF CONGRESS CONTROL NUMBER: 2016934926

Cover design by Laura Duffy
Book design by Astrid Lewis Reedy

Printed in the United States of America

Dedicated to
Anne Hastings and Gauthier Dieudonné

Contents

FOREWORD

In 1983, I was lucky enough to end up—through the serendipities of American privilege, although I was too young to know it—in the towns and villages of Haiti's Central Plateau. It was impossible to forget those first few months, and a little over a year later, I started moving between Harvard Medical School and Haiti. But one person, or even a handful of people, rarely if ever makes a difference in the fight against poverty and disease. In 1987, a group of us founded Partners In Health and a Haitian sister organization, Zanmi Lasante, in Boston and in Central Haiti respectively with the mission of providing a "preferential option for the poor in health care." We cribbed this idea from liberation theology, and borrowed other ideas—the importance of training and generating new knowledge—from academic medicine. Of course these ideas, and this quest for clinical excellence, were dealt a beating by the structural violence of rural Haiti, just as were the rural poor themselves. But these two organizations were shaped, as were all of us, by the experience and wisdom and trials—and sometimes the successes—of those we sought to serve.

It soon became clear that improving the health of our patients would require much more than the sundry medical supplies we could bring from Boston or purchase in Port-au-Prince. We knew we needed staff and stuff and space—a hospital, clinics—and spent long years recruiting, training, buying, and building. Since its start over 30 years ago, Zanmi Lasante has grown from a one-room clinic short on supplies to a staff of 5,700—nurses, doctors, other clinicians, community health workers, program managers, among others—across a network of hospitals and health centers, including a 300-bed teaching and reference hospital in the very same town in which we met in 1983—and a growing number of nurse and physician training programs. From Haiti to Russia, Rwanda, Liberia, the Navajo Nation and beyond, Partners in Health is working to build and rebuild health systems and train the next generation of health care workers.

Significant and sustained improvement in health outcomes also demands an interdisciplinary approach, one that addresses the social determinants of health. To do otherwise would be—to borrow from a Haitian proverb—like washing one's hands and then drying them in the dirt. Along with offering clinical services—which never feel good enough—we work to counter the structural forces that make and keep our patients sick. A doctor in Mirebalais may cure a patient of tuberculosis with a decades-old treatment regimen, but what then if poverty—usually a "pre-existing condition" among our patients—lands her back in the same poorly ventilated and overcrowded home in which she first got sick? A community health worker from Cange or Thomonde may accompany an HIV-infected patient through initiation of antiretroviral therapy, but what if he and his family go hungry from an absence of economic opportunity—a job, say, or a garden to till and the tools to do it productively—and no means of acquiring credit or access to financial services beyond the usury with which the world's poorest are grimly familiar? These examples are not abstract. As we've seen in settings from rural Haiti to the slums of Peru and post-conflict West Africa, in post-Soviet Siberia and in the Navajo Nation, access to adequate food, safe housing, clean water, and dignified employment are essential to health. That's why Zanmi Lasante and all of Partners In Health's sister organizations rely on community health workers (known in Haiti as *accompagnateurs*) not just to deliver medications to patients and link them to health centers, but also to help address the social and economic barriers that keep them from getting well.

It's also why we partner with Fonkoze, whose work to lift the most vulnerable out of destitution helps to protect them from the diseases that preferentially stalk the poor. Founded in Haiti in 1994 with a staff of five volunteers, Fonkoze, as Steven Werlin shows in *To Fool the Rain*, shares some of the same origins as Zanmi Lasante and Partners In Health. Since I'm lucky enough to know most of Fonkoze's founders, Haitian and American, I know that they too sought to make a preferential option for the poor, and that they too sought to serve and learn from the rural poor. Fonkoze has also experienced tremendous growth over the last two decades. Today, it is the largest microfinance organization in Haiti, having disbursed loans last year totaling over 28 million dollars; it currently serves over 60,000 borrowers and provides savings accounts for more than 200,000 Haitians. At its root, the mission of Fonkoze is not economic, but moral. Fonkoze's name is derived from the Haitian Creole phrase, *Fondasyon Kole Zepòl*, which roughly translates to "Shoulder-to-Shoulder Foundation." This name—Shoulder to Shoulder—is not one that would typically evoke a "bank" in the minds of its potential clients, but is illustrative of the radical approach of Fonkoze. The name rings familiar to Partners In Health, evoking a promise of accompaniment, a central theme of our work. This notion of accompaniment—standing shoulder-to-shoulder with patients or clients—eschews traditional notions of charity, and instead calls for pragmatic solidarity, an unconditional partnership with those in need. Fonkoze's reach extends to 45 branches across Haiti—nearly all of them in rural areas, and most of them isolated from commercial banks. This is not to mention its provision of other social services and amenities that are all too often absent from poor and rural locales. More than just geographic seclusion, Fonkoze works to break patterns of social isolation; 96 percent of its loans go to women. This resolute focus on addressing gender inequity—one of the most insidious and pervasive manifestations of structural violence—is essential to breaking cycles of poverty and disease.

That Partners In Health and Fonkoze have had such a fruitful and longstanding partnership, then, should come as no surprise. This partnership, spanning almost two decades, has integrated quality health care with pro-poor financial services across Haiti's Central Plateau and Artibonite Valley. In 2003, Zanmi Lasante and Fonkoze, together with Haiti's Ministry of Public Health and Population, established both a public hospital and a Fonkoze branch in Thomonde, replacing a crumbling clinic and bringing long-needed access to credit to the marginalized community. The same model was implemented in Boucan Carré a year later. This linking of services—medical and economic—was intentional, and stemmed from our joint mission to address the complex and interrelated social determinants of illness and poverty. Today, the hospitals in Thomonde and Boucan Carré serve a combined catchment area of over 120,000 patients, many of whom also participate in Fonkoze programs.

Following the success in Thomonde and Boucan Carré, Partners In Health and Fonkoze expanded our partnership: in 2009, with the support of the Clinton Global Initiative, Partners In Health and Fonkoze, together with other organizations, committed 50 million dollars over two years to bring our model of linking health care and social services to scale across central Haiti. The commitment linked sustainable enterprise through Fonkoze's micro-lending and cash transfers to the extremely poor, with comprehensive (and free) health services through Zanmi Lasante. Even at scale, the root of this model remains the same: pragmatic solidarity with the rural poor. Fonkoze's entry point to disrupting these cycles is its initiative called *Chemen Lavi Miyò*, "pathway to a better life." The program is an adaptation of a program developed in 2002 by BRAC in Bangladesh. It endows impoverished women with modest financial means to begin covering the costs of food, shelter and other necessities, including the materials to construct 9-by-9-foot homes with stable roofs, floors and latrines. Along with health care (provided by Zanmi Lasante), the women are given a small cash stipend to support an income-generating business, typically raising livestock or selling small goods. Each client is assigned a case manager to monitor and address her needs and provide training in skills related to her new business. As clients grow more stable economically, microcredit loans are available to individuals, and larger "solidarity loans" are offered to groups of five women to build their businesses. Today, this program embodies what is known as the graduation approach and is being adopted by governments and NGOs all over the world. Fonkoze has been a leader in this global movement.

ᘓ ᘓ ᘓ

In January 2010, the people of Haiti were dealt a devastating blow when a catastrophic earthquake struck Port-au-Prince. With nearly a quarter-million fatalities and significant damage to an already ailing public infrastructure, many existing aid and development efforts were either redirected or halted completely. Amid deep loss and grave challenges, Fonkoze never faltered in its resolve to support the most vulnerable, even in this most extreme circumstance. It was the only financial institution in Haiti to stay open in the days following the earthquake, giving its clients critical access to emergency funds and remittances. When the money ran low, two million dollars in cash from Fonkoze's accounts in the United States was transferred to its branches in Haiti—a complex and dramatic operation involving the United Nations, the U.S. Departments of State and Defense, camouflaged crates stuffed with cash, and a military C-17 helicopter. With its network of branches spanning across the country, Fonkoze was able to ensure that this money reached the most isolated and vulnerable clients far beyond Port-au-Prince. Access to these funds was crucial for clients in securing food, water and other basic necessities. *To Fool the Rain* thoughtfully chronicles Steven Werlin's journey with Fonkoze, but it is also the story of Fonkoze itself. The text offers historical and personal insight into the development of *Chemen Lavi Miyò*, an overview of Fonkoze's work in the communities it serves, and a focus on the improved lives of Fonkoze graduates. Presented in vivid detail are the lived experiences of Mirlene, Micheline, Ti Rizib, Monique, Rose Marthe, Alta, and other *Chemen Lavi Miyò* participants, who have benefited in many ways from this remarkable program. As Werlin makes clear in *To Fool the Rain*, there is no single pathway to a better life. We learn Mirlene's story of family tragedies and illness; despite this, she and her husband are planning next year's garden. Werlin describes the excruciating selection process for *Chemen Lavi Miyò*, telling the twin stories of the impoverished Monique and the more successful but still poor Mirlande. The stories of each of these women (and the other community members featured in this book) are the stories of Fonkoze: individual beginnings, challenges and successes bound together by the themes that pattern life in rural Haiti.

To Fool the Rain offers a window into the lives of Haiti's poorest. Just as Werlin describes the difficult topography that he traversed daily in order to meet with program participants, this book traces the geography of poverty that impacts health outcomes, educational opportunities and livelihoods in rural Haiti. However, Werlin also shares a powerful response to these inequities: Fonkoze's comprehensive programs, which offer financial services, classes, business skills trainings, and health services to the poor. At Partners In Health, we've long made the claim that poverty makes you sick. Lacking social safety nets, the poor in Haiti and elsewhere face ongoing and catastrophic cycles of poverty and disease. Fonkoze's pioneering work in solidarity with Haiti's poor has been a crucial step in disrupting such cycles. Fonkoze's model, particularly its *Chemen Lavi Miyò* program, offers a path to security and hope for marginalized women. In *To Fool the Rain*, Werlin limns pragmatic partnerships to end needless suffering, and gives encouragement and practical inspiration to all those who would seek to do the same.

—*Dr. Paul Farmer*

A NOTE ABOUT THE TEXT

Haiti has two official languages, French and Creole. In choosing how to spell place names, I followed a simple rule. For *komin*, which are like counties, I used French spellings: Thomonde and Mirebalais, rather than Tomond and Mibalè. I did this because I thought some of these names might be familiar to some readers. For places smaller than *komin*, I used Creole spellings, hence Mannwa and Bwawouj rather than Manoir and Bois Rouge.

Haiti and the Dominican Republic

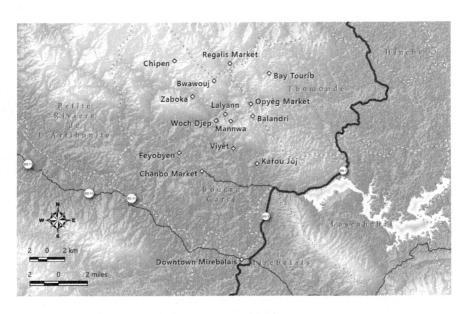

The area around Mannwa

PROLOGUE

The first time I saw Rose Marthe, she was more than eight months pregnant. It was midway through a hot tropical day, and I had hiked for a couple of hours to talk with her.

Her home was hidden behind a large tomb, on a small hill above the spot where the main path appeared to end its downward slant from the Mannwa ridge. The tomb had a good tin roof perched above it on a wooden frame. Someone wanted to make sure that its deceased inhabitants would be protected from occasional tropical downpours.

A larger *lakou*, a yard encompassing a small cluster of houses, sat close to the path on the right, and the hill with the tomb on it rose to the left. A couple of turkeys were wandering noisily around the tomb as I approached. A big male puffed himself up angrily at the sight of me, his comb turning from dark red to light blue.

Rose Marthe's dilapidated shack, built of sticks, palm leaves and mud, was set back beyond the tomb, behind a barrier of thorny succulents. It blended into the browning-green of the millet and pigeon peas planted behind it, so it was hard to see from the main path. Its roof was made of the pods from palm trees, rather than tin. These pods, called *tach*, can be almost six feet long and more than a foot wide. They're thick and fibrous. They provide some protection from the rain for a couple of months, but then they start to crack as they are alternately soaked by rain and dried by the sun. The roofing on Rose Marthe's house was long past cracked. She and her family lacked the protection that her neighbors were able to provide their dead.

When I arrived, Rose Marthe wanted to offer me a seat. Haitians, especially rural Haitians, attach a lot of importance to the way they receive visitors. Even a chance visit from a bare acquaintance is likely to lead either to an offer of food or drink, or an apology that nothing was offered. "*M pat ba w anyen*," or "I didn't offer anything," is something I constantly hear at the end of unannounced visits to poor households. It rings like a guilty admission that an unwritten law of hospitality has been broken.

Rose Marthe after 18 months

The very least that someone will do to welcome an unexpected guest is to position a good chair in the shade, so that the guest can sit comfortably. But Rose Marthe had no chairs. She had no furniture at all.

She tried to send her oldest boy across the small clearing to her neighbor's house to borrow a chair, but he was lethargic from hunger, so it was easy for me to sit down on the hard dirt, right in front of the door of her straw shack, before she could get him into motion.

She was shocked. *"Ou chita atè!"* she protested. "You're sitting on the ground!"

But sitting on the ground when meeting with women like Rose Marthe was what I had been trained to do. It is a way to manage one of the little embarrassments they are likely to feel when we first meet them.

I had been sent to see Rose Marthe by Fonkoze's *Chemen Lavi Miyò* team. My job was to determine whether she would qualify for a program designed to help the poorest of Haiti's poor families improve their lives.

ᛊ ᛊ ᛊ

It would be easy for me to feel out of place when I hike along the Mannwa ridge, with a broad view of the farmland of southern Boucan Carré to my left and the hills and valleys that stretch to southern Thomonde on my right, or when I sit in the dirt or on rocks in front of the huts, like Rose Marthe's, where Haiti's rural poor dwell. The world I share with the people I work with is a long way from the one I come from. Mannwa isn't very much like Lexington, Massachusetts.

Haiti is littered with Americans and other foreigners who say that they've fallen in love with the country. We come for a first short visit. Then we either stay or we start traveling back and forth, returning to visit over and over again. There's a lot to love about Haiti: beautiful beaches and a mountainous countryside; a handsome, generous and hospitable people; and a culture full of lovely and lively art and music.

I can point directly to the moment I first realized that I wanted to spend time in Haiti. It was during a visit to see a friend named David Diggs.

David had been an outstanding student in a philosophy course I taught in the early 1990s. He had come back to the United States after an initial experience working in Haiti. After finishing his master's degree in the States, he returned to Haiti to help found a very small organization committed to supporting education programs. David suggested that I come see what the country was like.

Haiti had been at the edge of my consciousness since I was a child. And my thoughts about Haiti were childish. I remember thinking it was funny that they would have a president called "Baby Doc." His fall in 1986, shortly after I graduated from college, had come across as something like a curiosity. Like the fall of Ferdinand Marcos that same year. I remember wondering ignorantly about the power attributed to his wife, Michelle Bennett, more or less the way I wondered how Imelda Marcos could have had so many shoes.

It was 1996 before I had the chance to visit. I spent a week with David, and he showed me around. I got to see some schools and meet some teachers.

The key moment was when David took me to an adult literacy center run by a nun from Quebec. It was housed in a primary school down in lower Delmas, a densely populated suburb north of Port au Prince.

Route de Delmas stretches from downtown Pétion-Ville at the top of the hill to a major commercial wharf near the bottom, splitting Delmas in two. The road is irregularly paved, gashed with an odd assortment of potholes large and small. From early rush hour until early evening, it's clotted with loud traffic. Men and boys weave through the cars, trucks and motorcycles, adding to the traffic jam, trying to make a few pennies from captive drivers. Some sell little bags of drinking water from sacks balanced on their heads or small bags of plantain chips. Smaller, poorer boys plead with drivers for the chance to smear their windshields with rags only marginally filthier than the ones they wear. Street merchants clog the narrow sidewalks, peddling suitcases, mangoes, barbequed chicken, used sneakers, batteries and padlocks, fried plantain, or Coke. They force the pedestrians— shoppers out to buy what they need to make their daily meal, children in their school uniforms, or men and women hiking up or down to work— to walk on the side of the road, clogging the traffic even more. The cars, trucks and buses that move up and down the road spew black and white smoke that mixes with pervasive dust to create air that feels thick, even when it's dry.

Four days each week, the literacy students—mostly large, middle-aged women—would push through Delmas' crowds of cars and pedestrians during the hottest part of the afternoon to a cinderblock school building, its tin roof efficiently radiating the late-afternoon heat downward into the classroom. There they would practice basic literacy drills, squeezing themselves into seats made for small children with their legs tightly folded under desks nailed to the front of the benches.

It was an uncomfortable place for me—noisy, hot and dusty—but I had been provided with a separate, full-size chair made of rough-cut wood and a seat of woven straw. It must have been much less comfortable for the women, pressed together as they were into their little, fixed benches.

They weren't complaining, though. They would shout their responses as we watched Sister Lise lead them through the questions and answers that passed for the consciousness-raising part of their program. They had come to the center to learn to read, but the literacy program was designed to teach them to think about the causes of their poverty and its potential solutions, too.

There I was, in the presence of women happy to have the chance to make the effort to learn, though they were packed into a dark room that was even hotter than the streets and alleys where they spent their long working days, squeezed into spaces made for bodies much smaller and more flexible than theirs. Their enthusiasm was contagious. They were participating in something wonderful that I wanted to be a part of.

So David and I started to talk about how I might be able to spend more time in Haiti. My first job out of college had been in western Alabama, helping rural teachers learn a way to hold regular discussions into their classrooms. The Touchstones Discussion

Project was created by some of my own teachers. David and his Haitian colleagues had long been thinking that they needed to help literacy teachers get their students more involved in their classes. He had even traveled to the States with some of those colleagues so that they could visit Touchstones classes, and see how the program worked. They all liked what they saw. So we decided that I would return the following summer, and spend two months helping a team adapt the Touchstones process for Haiti.

It was a wonderful visit. David's coworker, John Engle, found a place for me to stay with a Haitian family in Kaglo, a village in the mountains above Pétion-Ville. From there, it was a pleasant walk down to the city, so I could get to David's office whenever I needed to. At the same time, it was high enough up the mountainside that the nights were comfortably cool. I was surrounded by neighbors, especially curious young people who were anxious to talk with me, and that was just the support I needed to begin to learn Creole.

Over the course of the school year, David's team had translated some of Touchstone's materials and by the end of the summer, we were able to introduce a simplified version of the Touchstones process to a couple of groups of teachers. They seemed interested, so we left them to experiment over the course of the coming year. I returned again in the summer of 1998 to continue the experiment, and I spent a year and a half there in 1999 and 2000.

In January 2001, after almost a year and a half in Haiti, I went back to teaching at Shimer College, where I had been since 1996. I would return to work in Haiti each summer, but within a very few years, I knew that I wanted to go back for another longer stay. I had discovered that summers alone were not enough.

So I took another break from teaching at Shimer and moved back to Haiti in January 2005. My plans weren't very clear. I wanted to make contact with different organizations that might be interested in exploring participatory learning with me, and I decided to let myself be guided by whatever opportunities might arise.

One person who invited me to talk was Anne Hastings, the executive director of *Fondasyon Kole Zepòl*, or Fonkoze, Haiti's largest microfinance institution. Anne is an American, a former management consultant who had moved to Haiti to assist the founders of Fonkoze in the mid-1990s, shortly before I began visiting the country.

The organization was established in 1994 in the wake of the return to Haiti from exile of its elected president, Jean Bertrand Aristide. Aristide had won his office with a large majority, running at the head of a movement that promised hope and change for Haiti's poor. But he had been overthrown and was living in exile within a few months of his inauguration. Though he was eventually able to return, Fonkoze's founders came to believe that political democracy would never succeed in Haiti unless Haitians could build a more inclusive economy, and that they could bring more people into the work of economic development by establishing access to well-designed financial services for poor, especially rural Haitians who had had no access up until then.

The leader among the founders was Father Joseph Philippe, a Roman Catholic priest who both came from and served a rural parish in the mountains between Léogâne and Jacmel. Father Joseph believed that the key for Haiti's poor would be for them to organize themselves. Fonkoze reflects this fundamental conviction with its name. *"Kole zepòl"* means "put [your] shoulders together," so *"Fondasyon Kole Zepòl"* translates roughly as the Shoulder-to-Shoulder Foundation. The name emphasizes the solidarity it seeks to foster among Haiti's poor, solidarity that its founders felt would be crucial to the institution's success.

Father Joseph and Fonkoze's other founders had been able to agree on a vision and an approach, but felt they needed someone with strong management skills to bring that dream to life. Anne Hastings had come for a year, and was unable to leave. With her energy and ability to strategize, she won Fonkoze an international reputation for its commitment to the human goals of microfinance and its willingness to experiment with new approaches to achieving those goals. When Anne joined Fonkoze, it had a single office and a volunteer staff. Under her leadership, it grew into a nationwide operation with 46 offices, 60,000 borrowers, and a staff of over 800.

From its first days, Fonkoze was built to offer rural Haitians more than just banking services like loans, savings accounts, remittances, and currency exchange. Father Joseph and the others believed that poor women from rural Haiti would need more than cash to move their families forward. So Fonkoze offered its borrowers educational programs as well: basic literacy, business skills, and eventually other programs too. These programs were designed to complement financial services. I began working with Fonkoze by helping address some issues that the education programs were facing.

Stepping into to Anne's crowded office always meant descending into chaos. Her phone rang constantly. She was her own receptionist, and the institution's main contact with partners both in Haiti and abroad, so she was continually interrupting herself to take calls in Creole and English. Most of the important documents that ran through Fonkoze's main office required her signature. She had trained her staff to knock on her door and then walk right in, so a stream of employees would flow in and out with papers for her to read and sign.

But by weaving our way through the interruptions, Anne and I eventually got to whatever was on her mind. The first time we met, she explained a problem that the literacy program was facing. Fonkoze needed a way to make learning to teach literacy easier. She asked me whether I'd develop simple lesson plans and an approach to teaching literacy teachers how to use them.

It was the first of a long and varied list of assignments I took on for Fonkoze. Fonkoze is a compelling institution, and Anne is an exciting person to work with. She combines a willingness to experiment with an unclouded commitment to Fonkoze's mission. It seemed as though every time I stepped into her office, she was thinking out loud about a new challenge. And they weren't just intellectual puzzles, but opportunities to help poor people improve their lives.

At first, I helped only with the education programs, following through the initial assignment and then coaching and collaborating with Fonkoze's literacy team. But as Anne and I got to know each other, and as I got to know Fonkoze, I became involved in a much wider range of things. Anne is a little like Br'er Rabbit's tar baby: Every time I came in contact with her, I became more deeply stuck to Fonkoze.

I went by her office one day in early 2009, and she was meeting with her upper-level managers. She asked me to join the meeting, though my presence in her office that day hadn't been planned. That wasn't unusual. Most of my visits were unplanned, and she'd often have me sit in on meetings she was holding.

The group was talking about how to turn around several low-performing branches. Anne asked whether any of her senior staff members would be willing, at least temporarily, to give up their regular responsibilities at the central office to take over a bad branch.

She had addressed her question to the regular Fonkoze staff. I was still at that point an outsider, just helping out. I didn't work for Fonkoze. But a few days after the meeting, I asked her whether she'd be willing to give me a chance.

It seemed like a crazy idea, and not only because I lacked any relevant experience. For four years I had been wandering around a couple of different parts of Haiti, working with a range of partners, involving myself in a mix of urban and rural tasks as they happened to present themselves. I had worked with a group of rape victims in Port au Prince and a group of young men in a gang-controlled slum. I had been commuting to Léogâne to the south and to Lagonav, the large island across the bay from the capital, to work with school- and literacy teachers. And I had been traversing other parts of Haiti irregularly as well. I had three or four regular places to stay, and would spend nights in other odd corners my work happened to call me to. For the first time since I had begun working in Haiti, I was offering to settle for a time in one place without even knowing where that place might turn out to be. For people who knew me, it was a little hard to imagine.

Anne and her operations people sent me to the branch in Marigot, in southeastern Haiti, an important little port for commercial traffic between Jacmel and the Dominican Republic. The fish market at Marigot's wharf supplies restaurants, hotels and private residences in Jacmel and even Port au Prince.

I received a couple of days of training, but when I first got to the branch I was so obviously ignorant that my assistant was afraid to let me use the branch's database of loans, deposits and other transactions. He was sure that I would screw it up. I would repeatedly miscount and have to recount the piles of dusty, beat-up bills that our tellers would give me to verify at the end of the day. But I let the branch staff teach me what I needed to know about branch operations, I talked with Anne's staff in Port au Prince when I needed advice, and things at the branch got slowly back on track.

I worked in Marigot for more than a year. As my time there was ending, I was preparing to return to Shimer in September 2010. I had been in Haiti for over five years, through floods and an earthquake, and it seemed as though it was time to go home.

But one day Anne called me to her office to talk about CLM.

CLM is *"Chemen lavi miyò."* That means "the path to a better life." It's the name in Haitian Creole of a program designed to combat the extreme poverty that crushes the lives of the poorest of Haiti's rural poor.

Fonkoze had piloted the program very successfully, and had just received the promise of funding that would make a major scale-up possible. That scale-up would require inserting a new level of management between its director, Gauthier Dieudonné, and the case managers who work directly with families. Anne invited me to become one of four regional directors, and I couldn't refuse.

I knew something about the program. I had been invited several times over the years to translate for groups of visitors, and I had helped write some early drafts of funding requests.

The work promised to introduce me to a whole new world. Though I had learned a lot as a branch director about how market women manage their families with the very small businesses they run, those market women, though poor, were much, much better off than the families who enter CLM. The opportunity to be able to follow the program through its full eighteen months, and learn firsthand how it helps extremely poor families to comprehensively improve their lives seemed too good to turn down.

So I asked Shimer to give me a couple more years off, and I joined the team. Fonkoze sent me to Bangladesh for a month with the three Haitians who would be the other new regional directors. The four of us would be trained by BRAC, the institution that had invented the approach. By the end of June 2010, we were all in the field, among the poorest of the poor in Saut d'Eau and Boucan Carré, selecting new CLM members.

The view from the Mannwa ridge

PART I:

GETTING STARTED

Pi bonè se gran maten.

(Any earlier is dawn.)

Alta and her baby

≳ I ≲

Chemen Lavi Miyò

When I first met Alta, she was still in her teens. She was living with a much older man and her two daughters in Viyèt, a hilly area just northwest of Difayi, one of Boucan Carré's couple of towns.

She was a beautiful young woman, with smooth, light brown skin and small, clear eyes. Her older girl was a toddler, a little image of Alta, and the second was a baby, less than two weeks old, who had not yet been carried outside of the small shack. She hadn't yet even been named.

Just getting to the neighborhood was an adventure. Five of us made the trip. Three were new case managers— Sandra, Thermil, and Yvenette— and Wilson and I were new supervisors. We went on three motorcycles, but Wilson was the only experienced driver. He had been a Fonkoze loan officer in the Central Plateau when he first joined the institution, and had spent several years facing its bad roads every working day.

Each time we came to a pool of mud, we all got off our motorcycles and Wilson rode them across the mud, one after another. Two of the hills were especially difficult, with football-sized rocks of various shapes scattered closely throughout the slick, soft mud. Wilson would have to ride his own motorcycle over and around them. Then he'd come back for Sandra's, and then return for Yvenette and Thermil's. I hadn't yet learned to ride at all.

We left the bikes and split up, walking off toward the various houses on our lists to visit that day. Alta's little hut was a long way off the main trail. The footpaths leading to it were thick with dark mud and lined by walls of thorny cactus fencing. We picked our way through by stepping from rock to rock, turning and twisting to avoid the cactus spikes, but in some places we could do nothing but step right into the sludge. Local farmers we encountered had a better time of it than we did. They walked barefoot, some of them carrying their plastic sandals in their hands, whereas we'd have to stop now and again while one of us extracted a sneaker or a sandal from a deep spot of goo.

Viyèt stretches east to west as it rises from Kafou Jòj, and Alta was living in a small clearing on a slope that lies along the northernmost edge of Upper Viyèt. The steep hills leading up toward Gapi and Mannwa rise just across from the entrance to her *lakou*.

She didn't have a stick of furniture, so we sat on the ground in front of her shack. The day had been long already, and the sun was hot.

Alta mumbled almost inaudibly as she told her story. I had already been in the country for several years, and people would tell me my Creole was very good. But judgments like that mean little. I really struggled to follow her.

Creole is not a difficult language to learn to speak. I was expressing myself more or less, despite numerous mistakes, a limited vocabulary and bad pronunciation, within the first years of my experience in the country. But it's not an easy language to learn to understand, at least in its spoken form. The numerous contractions and the fast pace of ordinary speech make listening a challenge.

And listening to someone like Alta was especially difficult. I had learned my Creole in Pétion-Ville, where traditional Creole mixes comfortably with the French and English that upper-class Haitians speak. I had adapted to the language there quickly because of years of public school French. Hearing high school kids use words like "speak" and "enjoy," would make me smile. But it also helped me follow them.

But the Creole in Boucan Carré and other areas of rural Haiti is different. Rural Haitians use a different vocabulary and they speak with a different rhythm, especially in the area reaching from central Haiti to the north. They sing.

I couldn't hear Alta clearly, but I couldn't keep asking her to repeat herself. I was afraid it would lead her to clam up entirely. So I listened as closely as I could, cupping my hand to my ear to pick up as much of her mumbled whispers as possible. I don't know how much I really understood, but I slowly learned pieces of her story.

She was her mother's first child, and she didn't grow up at home. Dire poverty had forced her mother to send her to be raised by a wealthier neighbor, a woman who had a house and a business in Mirebalais, the closest major town. There, Alta grew up as a servant. She was never paid. She was not sent to school. But her guardian fed her and clothed her, which was more than her mother could do. Alta spent years with the woman, doing housework and helping her run her business. She would sit, crouched under the small, home-made table that her guardian would use to display her merchandise, ready to run errands or help make sales.

Then she became pregnant. The woman kicked her out, and her child's father abandoned her. She was left without a place to live. Her mother had just built a small house on her own father's land, and at first Alta just moved back in with her. Then she became pregnant again, and the second child's father also abandoned her. The old man decided to give Alta, his granddaughter, a little plot to live on. The man Alta was together with by then—who was not the father of either child—built them a small straw hut.

Life wasn't easy. The couple had no land of their own. The man could have worked other people's land as a sharecropper, but he had been sick during the planting season and so had failed to get any crops into the ground. He could do nothing but spots of day labor when his neighbors were working in their fields. Alta could do no heavy farm work that year because of her pregnancy. She had learned to run a business by watching the woman she grew up with, but without any money to invest she wasn't able to get started. The couple had no livestock.

What's worse, though she was dealing with a newborn and struggling to keep herself and her toddler fed, her childless partner was constantly pressuring her to have a child with him. "I just want to take care of the girls I already have," she complained.

The couple was hungry most of the time. Both throughout her pregnancy, as the baby was growing within her, and as she started nursing her girl in the days after she gave birth, Alta would wrap her stomach tightly with a scarf or a cloth before going to bed each night because she felt that it would relieve some of the hunger pangs.

꙳ ꙳ ꙳

That Haiti is the poorest country in the Americas and one of the poorest countries in the world is a fact almost too commonly known to be worth mentioning.

Its poverty can be described in various ways. One can consider the indicators that economists have traditionally used, like *per capita* income or *per capita* gross domestic product. Or one can look to more sophisticated, humane measures, like the United Nations Human Development Index, which attempts to capture how well or badly a population lives. But all the various measures paint a consistent picture of people who enjoy neither the wealth nor the standard of living of even the least of their neighbors. Haiti is roughly twice as poor as the other poorest countries in the Americas.

But statistics can do little to help someone understand extreme poverty. Knowing Haiti's *per capita* income doesn't prepare you for the day you meet a teenage mother who binds her stomach to suppress her hunger. Studying Haiti's Human Development Index says little when you're faced with a hungry, thirteen-year-old wage earner who has little chance of eating even one meal per day.

And such wealth as Haiti has is distributed unequally. At Pétion-Ville's Caribbean Supermarket, you can find products you'd look for at fine supermarkets in the States: freshly made sushi, French goat cheese, Greek olives, Italian vinegar, Californian raisins, flaky croissant, fine Chilean wines, and handmade sandwiches, garnished with pesto and fresh baby greens. The Caribbean is always full of customers—white, black and mulatto. They are missionaries and consular staff. They work for the United Nations or large, international NGOs. They may simply be members of one of a handful of the elite Pétion-Ville families who have dominated Haiti for generations, or belong to one of the Arab-Haitian families who have flourished in retail businesses for over 100 years.

Alta lives only a few hours from Pétion-Ville, but the Caribbean sells nothing that she could afford. And she wouldn't know that because it would not occur to her or to someone like her to step inside. And even if she did find herself there, she wouldn't know what to do. She'd be lost, not knowing how to look for things on its well-stocked shelves or to put her purchases in a shopping cart or to stand in line at a cash register while a machine adds up her purchases. The Caribbean is part of a world that does not have a place for Alta. More than 38% of rural Haitians live on less than $1.25 per day.

But most of that 38% are not what Haitians themselves would call "poor." The Creole word "*pòv*" is generally reserved for those whose state is really wretched. There is another word, "*malere*" for those who are merely badly off. Even very poor Haitians will rarely call themselves "*pòv*." It carries too heavy a stigma. Even middle-class professionals, however, might refer to themselves as "*malere*." Most of those living on less than $1 a day are *malere*, not *pòv*. At least until the next disaster strikes.

When things are going well, many such Haitians might manage to eat a decent meal every day. Maybe even two. A field hand can earn about $1 for a day's hard farm work, and that is enough money to buy what's needed to make what passes for a meal, at least in a small household: A small plate of low-grade rice for everyone, seasoned with a bouillon cube or two and slightly colored by a spoon or so of fried tomato paste. Chopped greens or leeks, or a pinch or two of dried herring, might be mixed in for flavor. Maybe even a few beans. A family might eat enough to stay reasonably healthy when there is work to be done in the fields. They might be able to ward off the worst hunger pangs. But these families are constantly at risk because of the fragility of the economic activities that sustain them. It's hard to have a backup plan when you're living on the edge. An illness, an accident, a little bad weather: it doesn't take much to turn a difficult life into misery.

To say that a Haitian family surviving on $1.25 per family member per day is not poor is in a sense to play a word game. But the word game has a point. The hard reality is that there are also lots of Haitians, many too many, whose lives are worse than bad.

They are landless, without crops to harvest or businesses to invest in or livestock to sell or consume, not to mention a job. They can go days without any income at all. They eat what they can, when they can. They might be a little better off during mango or avocado season, when they can scavenge abandoned fruit. Or during a harvest, when they might glean a cup of corn or millet in exchange for farm work in a neighbor's field or a heavy day of laundry. But they often go days at a time without ever having reason to light a fire under the triangle of three rocks that serves as their stove.

Their homes provide no shelter. Though the roofs offer some shade, those who dwell beneath them are sure to get soaked with every rain. Haitians have a way of describing such roofs. "*Yo ka twonpe solèy, men yo pa ka twonpe lapli.*" They can fool the sun, but they can't fool the rain. During heavy downpours, which can be almost daily in the tropics during parts of the year, parents will move their smaller children around on the floor, setting them down on whatever spots seem driest, sometimes finding a corner where the roof is more or less holding up, sometimes pushing them under the bed, if they have a bed. They might cover them with a tarp if they can find one, or they take them outside, collecting them under a tree that provides at least partial protection. The exposed roots of a mango tree might be drier than the muddy floor of the shack they call "home."

A house in Koray

Such families depend on cash income, either because they have neither land nor livestock they can subsist on, or because they cannot afford the seeds to plant whatever land they have. At the same time, most of the cash that they can earn comes from seasonal farm labor that is not only irregular but also astonishingly low-paid.

The children in these families lack educational opportunities because their parents cannot send them to school. But in a sense, that is the least of their problems because they regularly lack even food to eat. They can find themselves sent away, like Alta, to live outside of their families because their parents feel incapable of giving them even the least things that life minimally requires. And though one comes across stories of children who prosper in the homes they are sent to, one also hears stories of every sort of abuse.

These extremely poor households, often led by women, are locked in a cycle that starts bad and gets only worse.

And their extreme poverty is much more than the lack of assets and cash. The extremely poor are, to use a word that has perhaps gone out of fashion, downtrodden. They lack economic capital, but they lack social and psychological capital as well. They are friend-less, living in isolation even from their nearest neighbors. They lack vision, even hope. They are so caught up in the struggle to find food each day that they lose the habit of thinking about the days and years to come.

⇒ 2 ⇐

Finding Alta

Alta was just the sort of woman Fonkoze had been created to serve: a poor rural mother, unable to support her own family, much less participate in development. Fonkoze was offering credit along with educational services that would help women use credit well. And you might think that giving Alta access to credit would be just the thing to get her on her way. She had learned how to run a business in the years she spent helping her guardian in Mirebalais run one.

But Alta had a newborn and a toddler on her hands, and her shack in Upper Viyèt was a long hike from anywhere she would have been able to set up a new business. She was in no position to make use of a loan.

Others might fail in credit programs for other reasons. They might have too many children to leave capital in a business while little faces went hungry. Or they might lack the skills or initiative or imagination that even the smallest business requires.

Fonkoze came to realize that it was failing in a crucial respect. It wasn't reaching the poorest Haitian women. It was succeeding well with many poor women who were already managing small businesses. But it was failing with women who didn't yet have businesses or whose businesses were especially small. Such women could not generate enough income to both feed their children and repay their loans.

Fonkoze tried tinkering with its credit program, adding smaller loan amounts and extra support and training as a way to help poorer women succeed, and the results were encouraging. The new program, Ti Kredi, or "Little Credit," enabled thousands of previously excluded women to start developing small businesses. But there were still women who were simply too poor.

So the institution's leadership realized that they needed a way to help those families whom credit couldn't serve, those without other assets to fall back upon, those so incapable of managing their minimal daily expenses that a loan would almost certainly evaporate in their hands.

They would not, however, need to invent the approach. Anne Hastings was able to find what Fonkoze was seeking.

BRAC, a very large development organization, had already created a program called "Challenging the Frontiers of Poverty Reduction: Targeting the Ultra Poor." BRAC had been implementing the program in its home country, Bangladesh, since 2002. By happy coincidence, the BRAC team was at that very moment working with a unit of the World Bank to replicate the program in other countries, and Fonkoze was able to secure a place as one of the pilots. The folks at the World Bank agreed to try it in Haiti because they imagined that if it could work in Haiti, it could work anywhere.

The program's success relied on its comprehensive approach. It gave extremely poor women the assets they would need to establish small businesses. These assets were not loans, but grants. Then, it provided them with the training they needed to use those assets effectively. In addition, it helped them with home repair, sanitation, and access to safe drinking water. It also linked them to essential health care. It even created networks of social support in the communities that the extremely poor women lived in. Finally, and most importantly, it offered months of close, one-on-one coaching, helping the women learn to manage their assets, but also to live healthier lives.

Fonkoze used the Haitian government's poverty map to select the three poorest areas of the country – the western end of la Gonâve, Boucan Carré, and Trou du Nord in the northeast – and determined to serve 50 families in each area. It sent case managers and supervisory staff to Bangladesh to receive training from BRAC, and then welcomed BRAC staff to Haiti to assist with the program's adaptation. The team came up with a Creole name, *Chemen Lavi Miyò*, or "Pathway to a Better Life." The name was a way to point out that no one would be able to give a family a better life, but the team would help a family find its way.

The pilot was wildly successful, with 144 of the 150 families graduating after 18 months. Then, as now, graduation from the program was measured in relatively straightforward terms: Women left the program able to feed their family a substantial meal at least once each day. They had at least two income-generating activities and at least $150 worth of productive assets. Finally, they had a plan for the future and the confidence to know that they could succeed. In other words, they might still be very poor, but they were no longer living in misery. They were not *pòv*, but *malere*. And they had good reason to hope for even greater future progress.

Fonkoze knew that it would need to continue and even grow its version of the BRAC program. For a couple of years after the pilot, Fonkoze was able to keep up the momentum by raising the money to serve 100 or 150 families at a time. But the earthquake of January 2010 drew enough attention to Haiti that Fonkoze was able to raise the money to start working with 1,000 families. So we hired and trained a new, larger staff and began looking through Saut d'Eau and Boucan Carré to find the women, like Alta, whom we would serve.

≥ 3 ≤

Sorting through Index Cards

The Creole word "*blan*" is related to the French word "*blanc*," which means "white." The unique way that Haitians use the word makes sense in context. Most foreigners in Haiti are white, and in Haiti the word means "foreigner." Haitians call Asians "*blan*" as well. I once heard Haitians talking about UN police officers from Burkino Faso. The officers were much darker-skinned than most Haitians, but the Haitians I was with referred to them as the "*blan Afriken*."

I wear my foreignness in Haiti everywhere I go. It is a uniform that only slips into the background when I am with the Haitians who know me so well that they think of other things about me first. As I walk through most areas of Haiti, whether in the countryside or in Port au Prince, people call me "*blan*!" for all sorts of reasons. Sometimes they want to attract my attention so they can tell me something they think I need to know: "*Blan*, be careful, those dogs bite." Sometimes they want to ask me for something: "*Blan*! Give me a dollar!" Sometimes they want to say, "Good morning, *Blan*!" And sometimes they are children who simply want to yell, "*Blan*! *Blan*! *Blan*!" for no particular reason at all. When I walk home up the hill from Pétion-Ville to Kaglo, I can mark how close I am to my destination by listening to the way people stop calling me "*blan*" and begin to call me "*Mèt la*" – a title used for teachers – or simply "Steve."

Americans and other foreigners have been coming to Haiti for years bearing all sorts of gifts and doing all sorts of harm. My presence in the field when we first start to work in a neighborhood would be, at the very least, a distraction. Children would run toward me or away from me, according to the strength of their curiosity or their fear. They might point and yell, *"Blan! Blan! Blan!"* Or they might approach me with one of the two English phrases that many Haitian children know: "Give me one dollar" or "Good morning, teacher." Adults will often assume that anything a foreigner is connected to means giveaways, and their assumption will distort the information that our team needs. Or they will decide to avoid us entirely because I am part of the team. So I never get to go on the initial visits we make into communities to start our selection process.

Haiti is liberally sprinkled with extremely poor people, but that doesn't mean that the poorest of them are easy to find. Selecting the families who need the program is a complicated process driven by two separate, equally difficult challenges: to find the people who really need us, and to eliminate the families who don't.

And we have to get things right. The program costs a lot of money compared to Fonkoze's other programs. It takes more than $1,500 to finance each family, and the funds are entirely donated. The program generates no offsetting revenue. You don't want to burn through donated funds helping people who could be served with lower levels of support, support that might eventually pay for itself through the interest they would pay on a loan. But you don't want to miss anyone who really needs the program, either. Missing a family may condemn its members to continued misery. There aren't many other chances at a better life waiting for the families if we pass them over.

To further complicate things: when a program enters a poor community bearing what can only seem like gifts, decisions about who participates are charged. They are bound to stir up jealousies serious enough to affect the program's results and the lives of its participants. You can't eliminate jealousy, but you can mitigate it if you invite all of a community's members to participate in the selection process and can convince them that you have accurately chosen their poorest neighbors.

So we start selection by involving a whole neighborhood, and then send staff into the field to study the information the area's residents give us. As we begin working with the members of a community, we walk a fine line. On one hand, we know that a neighborhood's residents are the best source of information about the wealth and poverty of those who live around them. They know their own neighbors much better than we possibly could. We can't simply march in from the outside and assume that we will be able to figure things out by ourselves. On the other hand, we can't take the information that community members give us at face value. It almost always includes lies and other inaccuracies. Working with it involves a lot of checking and double-checking.

The process begins with a visit to the community. A couple of case managers go to a neighborhood that we plan to work in, and they walk around, trying to meet people and gain a sense of the lay of the land. They want to see where and how people live, and who the community's leaders are. They need to find out who can get people in the community to come to a meeting, because we go through two steps of our selection process at an open community meeting, and we want attendance to be good. We look for someone whose invitation to his or her neighbors will draw wide response. There is no mail service in rural Haiti, and many people are without cell phones. The best way to get the word out is to get it into the hands of someone who will talk with neighbors and encourage them to show up.

Since I cannot participate in these visits, I can only share the story that my colleague Hébert told me of one of his first site visits to a corner of southern Boucan Carré. He is an original member of the staff, having worked as a case manager during the pilot. When Fonkoze received the funds for the scale-up that would draw me into the program, he was promoted to be a regional director, and I met him when we left for a month of training in Bangladesh.

He was a great travel companion: curious and easygoing. He's a great colleague, too: smart, tolerant, and always good-humored. He laughs when something funny happens, but he often laughs when he encounters a surprising problem as well. It's very often his first reaction to both good and bad, and it helps.

Pajès is a long way from the center of Boucan Carré. The easiest way to get there is to take the main highway from Mirebalais toward Saut d'Eau. You reach a bend in the road that approaches the Artibonite River, and you cross the river in one of the dugout canoes that are its only ferries. Hébert made the crossing with Mystal, another member of the original team, and started strolling around.

Eventually they saw a guy who didn't seem busy, just relaxing in front of his home. So they went up to him and started to chat. His name was Miguel. They asked him about Pajès. First they talked about its shape, its extent. They asked him where it starts, where it ends, and what its little sub-neighborhoods are called.

As they began to talk more about the area – what and how its farmers plant, whether there are schools, where folks get their water – another man joined them. His name was Mauriceau. He had seen that Miguel was talking to a couple of strangers, and he wanted to know what it was about. He asked Hébert and Mystal what they were up to, talking like someone who had a right to know.

So they asked him to join their chat. By listening to Mauriceau and watching how Miguel interacted with him, Hébert and Mystal were able to see that Mauriceau was someone with authority. When Hébert asked him where people in Pajès go when they want to hold a meeting, he said, "They come to my house." Hébert and Mystal knew at that point that they had found someone who could get people together. Often, such a person is a local pastor or a school principal. Sometimes, a minor elected official is the one. Mauriceau was simply the largest local landowner.

Hébert didn't want to hold a meeting in Mauriceau's front yard. He was afraid that his assertiveness would become a barrier to broad participation. So they decided to hold that first meeting at a school instead. But they still asked Mauriceau to help them distribute invitations, and he did so to great effect.

Hébert smiles when he remembers the meeting itself. Mauriceau was there, but he wasn't comfortable in an environment in which everyone was encouraged to talk. He stood silently in the background, with his arms firmly crossed, taking it all in like a very strict father, allowing his children to have some fun.

We call the first part of that meeting "social mapping." Imagine 20 or 30 men and women, standing around an open space, talking. We ask them to trace a map of their neighborhood on the ground with a stick. We try to get them to argue with one another about all sorts of details, from whether the big mango tree is before or after the curve in the road to how many houses there are behind the old church. We make the procedure informal, encouraging everyone to get involved. And we get as many different people to take hold of the stick as possible by encouraging them to erase and retrace the necessary lines and shapes to correct one another's work. We ask them to place all the households in the neighborhood on the map, using index cards to mark the houses and writing the name of the head of the household on each card.

It's challenging work for our case managers; in most groups, one or two of the wealthier men will start to dominate. You have to keep your eyes out for people who seem as though they might want to talk, and then you have to get the stick into their hands quickly. Arguments about where to place a tree or a tomb or a stream are useful, if only because they get more people involved.

We don't let the participants know what the map is for. We explain as vaguely as we can that we were sent to collect information about the neighborhood. If people understand what our program will offer, we won't get good data. For an American like me, it's always a little astounding that rural Haitians will share as much information as they do with people they don't know, people who come with intentions that they can't be sure of. We only mention

Fonkoze if we find we need to. Often, we aren't even asked who sent us.

The two key results of social mapping are a pile of index cards with each family's name on one card and the map itself, usually quite stylized, which one of our case managers copies onto paper so that we'll have it in our files as we enter the next step in the process.

The case managers keep up an easy back-and-forth during the meeting to create a relaxed environment, one open to lots of give-and-take. When we turn to the index cards in the next step, people get into discussions that are charged and significant, so the environment must start out right.

We once held a meeting in Opyèg, a small market area hidden along the side of a valley near the border between Thomonde and Boucan Carré. The meeting got heated because a couple of the women present were afraid to have their names taken down. They were very loud about it. "Take my name off the list!" they kept shouting.

Another institution had passed through the area a few months earlier, and one of their staff members was a young man with a snake tattoo on his arm. Though none of us had tattoos, we were, as strangers, guilty by association. We were close to neighborhoods where case managers trying to do initial site visits had been threatened with machetes, so the situation was volatile.

But the case manager who was running the meeting was Anselet, a tall man with a low voice and a slow way of speaking. The sound of his Creole, with the musical drawl of his home in northeastern Haiti, was amusing enough to these Haitians from the lower Central Plateau to put them at ease. But he also kept up a steady patter of funny little quips – flirtatious, but also self-effacing – while he continually asked participants to verify and correct one another's work. He had created such a friendly rapport with most of the people present that some of the participants who were enjoying the meeting were willing and able to cool their neighbors off.

Anselet copying the map of Opyèg onto paper

The next step in the selection process is called "participatory wealth ranking." It's where we use the stack of index cards to help a community identify its poorest households, the ones that need our help most.

A case manager starts by taking the top two cards from the stack and asking participants which of the families represented by the cards is wealthier. This can involve a lot of disagreement. If we have failed to create the right environment, the discussions that ensue can be hard going. One or two individuals can dominate. Or the whole group can be reluctant to talk. But if the first part of the process has gone well, the second part tends to go well too.

If the group decides that the two families are about equal, we put their index cards into a single pile. If one of the families is wealthier than the other, we start two different piles. Next we take a third index card and ask the group to compare this third family with the other two. We go through the whole stack this way, aiming to end up with about five separate piles that represent the different ranks of wealth that the community divides itself into.

We then ask the group to spend a few minutes thinking about each pile and identifying the criteria that define its members while they check to see whether there are any names that seem to be in the wrong pile. What are the common threads that distinguish wealthiest members of the community? What distinguishes the poorest families from the next-to-poorest? We transcribe what they say, and so have a record of the way each community evaluates wealth.

The criteria they come up with can vary, but they do not tend to be surprising. The wealthiest families might be the ones who send their kids to university, they might have several cows, they might own more than a couple of large pieces of land, or they might have their own cars or trucks. They hire groups of day laborers to help them farm. The distinction between the poorest and the next-to-poorest might be that the poorest are entirely landless, they have no goats, and they have to work as day laborers or beg just to have food to feed their kids.

While none of the rural Haitians who attend these meetings compare with the men and women who visit Pétion-Ville's Caribbean Supermarket, there are nevertheless enormous differences among them. Families with large land holdings, who can harvest much more than they consume, devote plots of their land to cash crops like beans, plantains or sugarcane. They can further increase their wealth by investing profits from their harvests into large businesses. They might buy up produce to add to their own crops, and sell it by the truckload in Port au Prince. Or they might invest in goods like gasoline or construction materials, selling them in and around the larger towns.

Less successful families will have smaller farms and smaller businesses. But they'll still manage well, sending their children to decent schools in large towns like Mirebalais and Hinche, and even to Port au Prince when they are ready for college.

The rural middle class consists, again, of farmers. But these farmers have only one or two plots, and their little retail businesses earn just enough to keep them and their children decently fed. But a single serious illness or the funeral expenses that a death implies can send them into misery.

Of the five or so piles of index cards, the ones that matter to us are the two at the bottom because our job at this point is to find the poorest families. We verify the second-to-poorest pile in addition to the poorest because we know from experience that we cannot rely on the results of wealth ranking. They give us a good starting point, but there are always families misplaced on the lists.

To make our preliminary selection of new members, we use the list of names and the maps that show us where each family lives. Case managers go out in pairs and interview the adult woman of each of the households in the bottom two categories. They use two surveys that help us define each family's level of poverty. One is Fonkoze's own poverty scorecard. It collects information about four different areas of a woman's life. We ask about her house and the land it's on, her productive assets and any significant possessions she owns, her income and where it comes from, including whether she has a husband or partner who contributes, and about various personal things like the size of her family, her education, the food she eats, and the water she uses. The scores can range from zero to 63.5. Scores under 20 generally attract our consideration.

The second form is called a "food security index." Case managers use it to divide families into three categories: food secure, food insecure, and food insecure with hunger. The families we are looking for fall into the last group.

But case managers don't just ask questions and write down responses. They also observe. That's one of the reasons they work in pairs: one speaks with the woman while the other listens to her answers, takes notes, and looks around.

When we were looking for new members in central Boukan Carré in 2010, two of our case managers, Sandra and Yvenette, went to visit a woman named Marie Lourdes.

Sandra is a large, tall woman, with dark skin, broad cheeks, and large, bright eyes. She's rugged. I learned a lot about what it takes to ride a motorcycle on irregular, unpaved trails by watching her fall, swear mildly, and then simply lift up her motorcycle and continue on her way with blood trickling down her forearm. She loves playing with the children she encounters. Alta's daughter would always sit on Sandra's lap while Sandra and her mother met, and if the little girl didn't fall asleep before they were finished, she would scream and cry when Sandra started to leave. Sandra would then have to carry her to the next house she had to visit, and leave her sleeping there.

Marie Lourdes was a single mother living in Chimowo with her seven children. Yvenette sat and talked with her while Sandra took the survey forms, and got out of Marie Lourdes' field of vision so she could look around. Yvenette's work would be easier if she could just talk, without having to write, so part of Sandra's job was to listen and take notes. But she was also observing, seeing the answers to questions that the two of them would thus not even need to ask.

But the kids surrounded her.

At first, they were just curious. They had never seen the women before, they weren't used to visitors, and were wondering what it was all about. But Sandra knew that they could make Yvenette's job difficult if they became a distraction for Marie Lourdes. So she tried to keep their attention even as she listened to Yvenette's interview and made her own observations.

The kids were smart. Even without seeing what stood in the forms, they could tell that Sandra's notes related to what their mother was saying. But by keeping them entertained, Sandra made it possible for Yvenette to do her job.

Case managers look especially for signs of hunger. They look at the cooking area to see whether it appears used. In rural Haiti, the typical stove is a simple triangle made of three rocks. The pot sits on the rocks, and the cook pushes sticks – usually just dead branches culled from whatever trees or bushes that are nearby – underneath the pot to provide the fire. When the food is done, the cook pulls the remaining wood out from under the pot, and leaves it near the stove, ready for the next meal.

It's easy to tell whether the stove has been used recently: one looks for traces of unburned wood and ashes. A triangle of rocks with a charred, black spot in the middle but no sticks and no ashes hasn't been used in a while.

Case managers also try to identify what sort of pots and pans there are for cooking. A family of six that has only a single small pot to prepare meals in probably is eating poorly.

And they consider whether the younger children are hanging around and whether they look hungry. Adults may hide hunger. Children generally don't.

Where I grew up, being hungry meant that food was on the way somewhat later than you had hoped or that you hadn't liked the last meal so you hadn't eaten as much as you could have. We used to say that we were "starving," but we really only meant that we hoped we'd be eating soon or that we wanted one of our favorite snacks before it was time for a meal.

Hunger in Haiti is real. I remember the first time I realized that. I was with my American friend Erik in Gwojan, the community where he was staying to learn Creole in late 1999. We were chatting with one of his poorer neighbors. Her deaf boy was running around noisily, playing soccer by kicking an empty can up and down a small hillside. I casually mentioned how much happy noise the boy was making, and her response stunned me enough that I still remember it almost exactly. "He ate well yesterday, so he has lots of energy today." I was talking with a mother with enough experience of hunger – her own and her boy's – to see clearly the effect of the occasional decent meal she could provide.

When we are visiting families who might qualify for our program, the sight of idle, lifeless children, too hungry to play, is a regular part of our day. Younger children are noisy, made angry by the pangs of hunger they feel. Or they are lifeless, too hungry even to misbehave. Older children are entirely absent, either scavenging for whatever unclaimed fruit might be lying around their neighborhood or hanging around neighbors' homes, hoping to get a spoonful of food when their friends' mothers serve a meal. Haitians say, "*Manje kwit pa gen mèt.*" That means that food, once it has been prepared, belongs to no one in particular. And it is the rare Haitian mother who won't find a half-plate of food for an extra child who appears around lunchtime, and the rare Haitian child who won't give a friend a couple of spoons of food from his or her own plate.

When this part of the process is complete, we have lists of families that our case managers have recommended for the program. But we go through a second level of verification to double-check whether the families we've found are really the poorest of the poor.

⇉ 4 ⇇
Final Verification

Monique is the widowed mother of six kids. They live in Danton, a hilly, heavily farmed neighborhood of eastern Saut d'Eau. She was once a market woman and had started to thrive. As we sat together in a shaded corner behind her small house, she explained how her business had grown strong enough that she had begun buying livestock out of the profits.

She and her husband were watching their household begin to flourish when disaster struck. He became sick, lingering but constantly weakening for five years. In an effort to save him, they spent what they had, first selling off the livestock they had managed to accumulate and the land they farmed, and then using up the capital that was in Monique's business. Nothing helped.

He died about five years before we met her. She had planned to sell their last piece of land, the small yard that the house sits on, to pay for his funeral, but her neighbors convinced her not to. Instead, they chipped in for the funeral themselves. One of them even gave her the use of a small plot of land right next to her house so that she'd have something to farm.

This brings me to her oldest boy, Jean Ken. When we met him and his mother, he was an important wage earner in the household, though only about 13 years old. Their main source of income was what he and Monique earned working in other people's fields. Between mother and son, they might make about $1.80 for a day's hard work. And that was on good days. They couldn't count on finding work every day.

Jean Ken sat scowling in a corner of the yard as I spoke with Monique. She explained that her boy had spent a couple of hours, starting early in the morning, planting sweet potatoes on their borrowed plot of land. It was hard work, and he was hungry. She had told him that he would have to wait. She had some corn lying in the sun on a sheet of rusted corrugated tin. A neighbor had brought the corn by as a gift, but Monique said that she would have to dry it out before grinding it into meal. When I asked her how long that would take, she said that it would be ready the next day.

It was early afternoon, and I was starting to feel hungry. But my meal would be waiting when I got back to Saut d'Eau. Neither Monique, Jean Ken, nor her other kids had any prospect of eating that day.

I met Monique as part of the process of final verification. Everything she said and everything I saw as I looked around her yard marked her family's need for the program. Her children weren't in school because she couldn't afford to send them. They sat around her yard, cranky and lifeless with the hunger that gnawed at them. What's worse: the school they couldn't afford to go to had a free lunch program that would have ensured them daily meals.

Final verification is the last step in the selection process. We take the list of families that our case managers have recommended to us, and we have someone from our management team interview each of them at home. It might be our overall director, Gauthier, or one of the regional managers, like me.

This is the moment in the process when I first get involved in the field, when I start to meet potential members. Up to now, I've been in the background. The rest of our team's management can dive in at every stage.

But final selection brings me into the field. I go out with a case manager who has done the preliminary selection in a neighborhood as my guide, and we hike from one home to another, chatting with women to see whether they qualify for our help.

The first time you step into a yard to see whether someone is poor enough to be part of our program, you don't quite know what to do with yourself. It is uncomfortable for the woman you're interviewing because she is not used to visitors and is unhappy that she cannot offer you even a comfortable chair. And it's awkward for you because you're sensitive to her embarrassment and conscious of the hunger that surrounds you.

You try to get a sense of a woman's story. If you can understand the narrative that underlies a family's poverty, you can make more reliable judgments about it. For some families, like Alta's, poverty is all they have ever known. It has shaped everything about their lives. For others, it is the result of one or more disastrous twists of fate. Monique and her husband had been succeeding, but his sickness and death cost them everything they had. A short conversation with Monique was all I needed to be convinced that she and her boys belonged in our program.

But there are cases like Mirlande as well. I met her the first time I went out with Gauthier, learning the verification process from him. We had been going from house to house together. He was watching me interview women, sometimes whispering a few words of advice in English as he listened in. By the time I got to Mirlande's house, however, I was working on my own. We would each interview a woman, then we'd meet and share notes before going on to the next two homes.

Mirlande is a young mother of five. She's a lively woman, and was smiling and chatty throughout our interview. She was living on a hillside just southwest of downtown Saut d'Eau. Her home was made of woven strips of wood covered with a layer of mud. Its roof was made of *tach*. It had a dirt floor, and lacked even a very basic latrine. She shared it with her kids and the man who is father to the four youngest ones. The seven of them were living on what the father could bring in by farming. He would also buy pigs on credit and resell them without leaving the market so he could repay what he borrowed by the end of the day. They didn't have the means to get into the more lucrative business of raising the pigs themselves. That would have required the capital both to buy the pigs clear and invest in feed.

Mirlande and her husband had a working, though volatile partnership. They did not own the land they were living on. They were renting the house and the land it stood on, including a small plot next to it that they farmed. But they also owned two pieces of land, a smaller one her husband inherited from his father, where they were starting to build a house, and a larger one they bought when her husband sold a cow. Her three oldest children were in school. The first had his tuition paid by his father, who supports him in no other way, and the other two got in through a kind of buy-one-get-the-next-two-for-nothing arrangement. They were regularly eating about once a day, feeding on the millet and corn that they would harvest for as long as that lasted and then on what they could buy with earnings from the pig trade.

I doubted neither Mirlande's poverty nor her need. I knew that she and her family were occasionally going hungry. They were leading a terribly hard life. But the structure of support that her husband could provide, including a regular if inadequate source of income and the capacity for future planning that their purchase of land demonstrated, at least suggested that credit might work for her. So I went back to Gauthier, and told him that I didn't really think Mirlande needed us. She was very, very poor, but not quite poor enough. I described her struggles, hoping that Gauthier would tell me to let her into the program after all. Or that he would at least go back to her with me and decide whether I was right or wrong.

It was the first time I was inclined to go against the case managers' recommendation, and it felt strange. It was hard to trust my own opinion. All the case managers are Haitian, and part of me wanted to assume that they must know better.

But Gauthier wouldn't help. He is not inclined to take back

responsibility once he's delegated it. He said that I had to make the decision I thought best and stand behind it. That was my job. So I took Mirlande off the list for CLM.

It isn't the kind of decision one can feel good about, even if it seems correct, because it robs a very poor family of resources that could do its members an awful lot of good. But we need to reserve those limited resources for the families who need them most because as it stands, there are many more of them in Haiti than we can possibly serve.

As I was signing the form that would lead to Monique's membership, I found myself staring at Jean Ken, her hungry, hardworking boy. I couldn't take my eyes off him. He sat alone, under a tree overlooking an incline in the farthest corner of his mother's *lakou*, gazing angrily and hopelessly into the distance.

So before I left her yard, I had one of her younger boys tell Jean Ken that I needed to talk to him. He came over, sullen but obedient, and I handed him 100 gourds. I asked him to give it to his mother to buy food to prepare a meal. As I walked away, the younger boy ran past me. He was, presumably, on his way to a local merchant to buy rice and the couple of other basics that would make up a simple meal.

Part of me was embarrassed by my gesture: Giving out loose change might feel good, but it wouldn't solve Monique's problems. Tomorrow and the next day, she and her children would face hunger again. I knew that help was on the way because I had chosen her for our program, but she would still be managing her children's hunger for some time to come.

And when we're out in the field, we can't make a habit of handing out little bits of cash wherever we see a need. The needs are all over, and creating expectations can tend to make our work even more complicated than it already is. Giving cash to people we hardly know isn't Fonkoze's approach. We are not a charity.

But we can't always do the principled thing. Sometimes we do what our hearts tell us. It makes a difficult job easier on our souls.

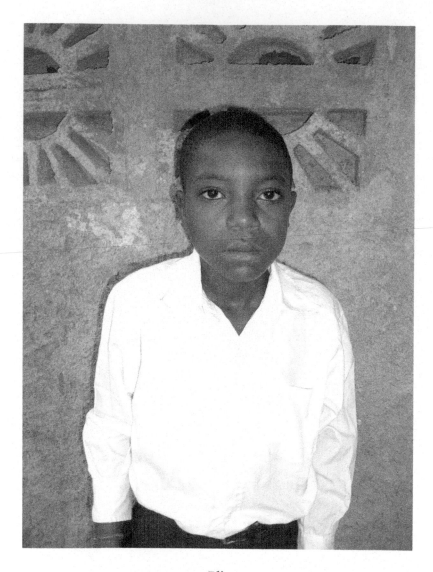

Elie

⇒ 5 ⇐

Walking with Elie

Almost as soon as we decided that our first expansion of the program would be in Saut d'Eau and Boucan Carré, we made a commitment to work in Tit Montay. It's the westernmost of Boucan Carré's sections, and the least accessible part of the south-western Central Plateau. One of the regional managers, Bethony Jean François, had hiked up a few years earlier for some other work, and had been struck by the isolation and the poverty.

We were just starting the scale-up in the summer of 2010, and we were audacious. Our mission was to eliminate extreme poverty in the Central Plateau, and we liked the idea of proving that we could go to its most remote and difficult corner first.

I had been out of the country for two weeks as we prepared to start selecting families in Tit Montay, and by the time I got back, the team was hard at work there. Before I left, we had agreed that I'd join them as soon as I got back. Since I didn't know the area, I had to hire a local man to guide me up to Zaboka, the largest village in Tit Montay's eastern half.

I was very foolish as I prepared for the long hike that would take me there from Chanbo, the town in the center of Boucan Carré. I packed more clothing than I'd need into my backpack. But more importantly, I piled in some peanut butter to share with the team and a couple of books. It was all stuff that would be nice to have with me, but it was heavy. I am not a big, strong man, and I lacked the experience and humility to recognize that I should make my load as light as I could. I had filled a large backpack and a second bag as well for a weeklong trip, and I was a long way from Zaboka when I began to feel their weight.

The first part of the route from Chanbo to Zaboka is an easy hike through a hilly, grassy landscape. Then it reaches a mountain stream. It winds upward along the stream to a waterfall, where it turns into a thin trace, scratched into solid rock. A series of small, cupped footholds allow someone to scramble up using hands and feet. But pack animals – horses, mules, donkeys – can't make the trip. They either go over the higher, but easier, ridge that passes through Belepe, or they take the much longer path over and around Mannwa.

I arrived in Zaboka early in the afternoon, only a little the worse for wear. It was early enough that I was able to catch my breath, leave my things at our base, and set off with a case manager to interview some women. The three other regional directors – Bethony, Hébert and Wilson – had already been in Tit Montay for over a week with more than a dozen case managers. They had done most of the work on the Deniza side, selecting and verifying potential members, and had moved on to Bouli. But they left three case managers behind them in Zaboka to visit the women they had missed the first time they had gone looking for them. And I would verify the case managers' recommendations when I arrived.

Zaboka sits in the middle of Deniza, the region that comprises the whole eastern half of Tit Montay. Deniza is thickly threaded with steep, rocky ravines. Hiking around is hard work for those unused to it. But it's also a populous area with several small villages and plenty of households scattered throughout the farmland that spans the slopes that separate them.

The team that went on to Bouli had left me a general plan for the couple of days of work that remained. On my first day, I was supposed to hike to Mablanch, Pay Diri, and two or three other neighborhoods well over an hour away from the base. I would go with Lénort. We only had about a dozen homes to visit, but they were scattered widely throughout Deniza. The list consisted of a household or two in each neighborhood.

It would be a long day of hiking around, and I was chagrined when I learned that Jean Romain would not be available to join us. He needed the day to take his daughter down to Chanbo so that she could be measured for her school uniform and he could pay her school fees. A tiny girl, she was to start kindergarten, and she would move into the house that her young aunts and uncles share while they attend school.

Jean Romain was the newest member of our team. When we decided to enter Tit Montay, we thought that working in so remote a region would be much easier if we had someone on the team with local knowledge. So we hired Jean Romain. He grew up in Zaboka as the son and grandson of important local leaders, and he quickly became a key to our work.

He is short, like most rural Haitians, but he towers over his father and grandfather, who are both squat, muscular men. His father, Nava, is a local Partners in Health community health worker and was our link to Jean Romain. Nava is also the lay leader of the village's large Baptist church and an important local healer, with advanced knowledge of traditional remedies like herbs and massage and how to set broken bones. Jean Romain is much thinner and quieter than his father, whose explosive laughter is a constant in the already loud *lakou*. The younger man is reserved, with a dark, narrow face and a small beard, but he's friendly and relaxed, with an easy smile. He had been leading case managers around to the various neighborhoods of Deniza, helping them plan initial community meetings. His father's name made him credible wherever he appeared.

Without him, I thought our trip to Mablanch would be a miserable affair. We could have used the maps that were produced at the wealth ranking sessions to find the families we needed, but that would be challenging because the maps tend, in the best of circumstances, to be only moderately accurate and would surely be less so in Deniza, where the irregular terrain makes mapping especially hard.

There are no roads in Tit Montay, only footpaths. At the peak of the fall harvest, in a year that had had plenty of rain, the paths were almost invisible to anyone who didn't know them. They were entirely overgrown with the grasses that cover uncultivated areas. Much of it is *zèb ginen*, which can grow well over six feet high. Without a guide, we weren't going to get very far.

Jean Romain, however, showed no sign of concern. He would send us with Elie, his brother.

Jean Romain is 29, his parents' eldest child. Elie is their youngest. He's 11, and doesn't look a day older than that. So when Jean Romain told us that Elie would be our guide, I was skeptical.

Elie is short like most of his family. He has his father's light skin and bright eyes. I had never heard him say more than *bonjou*, *bonswa*, and *wi*. Children in the Haitian countryside are taught not to talk in the presence of adults.

Lénort and I called for him when we were ready to leave the next morning, as soon as we had eaten the boiled plantains that Jean Romain's wife had made for us. Elie appeared immediately. He had gotten up early, afraid to keep us waiting. He was wearing old jeans, a t-shirt, and a pair of flip-flops. Not exactly hiking gear. He stared at the ground as Lénort went over the series of neighborhoods we'd need to visit. A Haitian child won't look a grown-up in the eye. He seemed every bit the little boy he was.

I had my doubts. But I didn't see any alternative to giving him a try.

I reminded myself that children grow up differently in different cultures. An American child is not a Haitian child. And even within Haiti, there can be big differences in the various ways that children grow up, differences that greatly affect what they are able to do and when. But I was still surprised to find myself facing the assumption that an 11-year-old would be able to guide two strangers through

various mazes of footpaths in areas well more than an hour from
his home, able to hike with us uncomplainingly for over six hours
through bright sunshine and heavy rain. He would have to lead us
to the homes of people he didn't know, people who wouldn't even
know who he was until he mentioned his father.

But that's what Elie did: speaking only when spoken to, waiting
patiently for Lénort and me when we fell too far behind. We would
lose him occasionally because the grass was so far over his head.
In places, it was over mine, too. Then we'd have to yell for him to
circle back to find us. Lénort gave him his canteen of water to carry.
When it wasn't raining, the sun was hot. But Elie didn't take a sip
until Lénort thought to offer him a drink. Then he gulped down
quite a bit. He had been thirsty, but hadn't presumed to speak up.
We hadn't brought food with us, so we went hungry throughout the
day, except for the fragrant wild guavas we would occasionally pass
on the sides of the trails. Guavas are not a cash crop, so people feel
free to pick and eat any that they come upon.

But Elie hiked uncomplainingly through it all.

When we returned to his parents' house, he was giddy, pleased
with himself for having discovered a series of little paths that he
hadn't known about before. His parents listened patiently while
he explained the shortcuts he had taken, and they smiled at his
excitement.

Elie is in school. He was scheduled to leave Tit Montay the following week for his family's apartment in Chanbo, where he would
spend weekdays throughout the school year, the same apartment
that would be home to a couple of brothers and sisters and their
niece, Jean Romain's little girl. He could hike home some weekends,
but he told me that he planned stay down in Chanbo most of the
time. The five-hour hike home is long.

Apparently, he's a rotten student, having repeated several classes
since he first went off to school. But growing up in Zaboka has given
him knowledge and ability that school does not measure.

≥ 6 ≤

Micheline

Most of the women we recruit to join *Chemen Lavi Miyò* accept our invitation, but some refuse. And even those who accept usually do so without enthusiasm. They don't really believe what we're telling them when we explain the program. It sounds too good to be true. They join, but only because just going along with what an authoritative-looking person suggests to them must seem like the easiest thing to do.

Haiti is littered with development projects and charity give-aways, but even if a woman we select lives in a neighborhood that has seen its share of offerings, she has probably not taken part. One of the most common characteristics of extremely poor people is an inability to nose their way to the front of a line. They often lack the initiative it would take just to get into a line at all. Their better-off neighbors are better off, in part, because they know how to claim advantages for themselves or they have others who will direct advantages to them.

And even if a woman has been included in a project, the experience may only have left her with further reason for doubt. She may have had the chance, for example, to be part of a cash-for-work program. Cash-for-work has been common in the Central Plateau and elsewhere in Haiti, especially in the years following the earthquake of 2010. Funders think of the projects as killing two birds with one stone. They improve local infrastructure while they get money into the hands of people who need it. Typical pay for a day's work is Haiti's minimum wage – 200 gourds, or a little less than $4.50 – to do basic things like digging roads with shovels and picks or protecting hills from erosion. But often participants sign for their 200 gourds, then actually receive much less. The community leaders who manage the payroll will take a cut, feeling entitled to it for having provided each worker their job. Or they will give the jobs to well-to-do friends, who wouldn't consider doing such work, and these will send poorer neighbors in their place, giving them just a portion of the daily wage. So when we come along, looking as though we might just be another project, they look at us, and they wonder.

Some women hesitate to join our program because of the weird things that they have heard. As soon as our team starts working in a region, rumors of the most curious sort begin to spread. A woman named Perrona, who eventually joined us, told me that she had refused at first because she'd heard we would make her dance naked. We have heard that we distribute magic turkeys that give birth to serpents, that we would be marking members "666," and that we would keep a second key to the house we'd help them build. Jealous neighbors come up with stories to tell potential members. They lie to discourage them from taking advantage of the program, and their lies are most striking for the inventiveness they display.

So jealousy is one problem. The way we threaten existing power relations is another. The program can undermine the usual order of things in two ways. There is an economic order in the Haitian countryside. Large landowners benefit from the cheap labor that their poor neighbors provide. These latter have little choice but to accept work for only a quarter of the Haitian minimum wage because they have no other way to feed themselves and their kids.

There's also a sexual order. Men dominate poor households in part because their children's mothers have no way to earn money on their own. They sometimes feel threatened by the prospect of a woman building the independence that having a separate livelihood could bring.

It was especially difficult to get women to agree to join us in Mannwa. Over half of the families there who qualified for the program refused to join.

By the time I first went there, I had been part of the team for several months. At first, we had focused our efforts in Saut d'Eau, in the Central Plateau's southwest corner. We were selecting 1,000 families, and we wanted to get a first group started as quickly as possible. So our team had worked together closely, focusing on the one region, facing every challenge together. I would head into the field for final verification with other managers. Each of us would have a case manager to guide us, and we'd meet together to exchange notes and share snacks throughout the day.

Then we moved on to Boucan Carré. I started to see less and less of Wilson, as he began to focus on getting things started in Saut d'Eau. Bethony began to spend most of his time in the area around Bouli, the remote area in the western side of Tit Montay. So a wide swath of Boucan Carré was left to Hébert and me. We had yet to decide which of us would be responsible for each neighborhood, so we worked together. It felt good. Hébert was a security blanket. He was experienced in all aspects of the program, and he never minded helping me out.

Mannwa was the first neighborhood that I managed on my own. It is hard to get to, sitting along one of Boucan Carré's higher ridges. No roads lead up to it, and no good roads lead even to its base. A trip to Mannwa is an all-day affair, and our case managers had found too few families there to justify a full day of final verification for both Hébert and me. So I hiked up to Mannwa with a case manager to verify selection by myself. Then I went back with Lénort to help invite the women we had selected to join the program.

When several families declined the program, we organized a meeting for community leaders. I hiked up a third time, this time with Sammuel, one of the case managers, to talk with them. We hoped that they would help me convince their poorer neighbors that there was nothing to fear.

Sammuel and I stood in a circle in a small shaded clearing with about a dozen local farmers, middle-aged men carrying the machetes that Haitian farmers rarely appear in public without. He introduced the two of us and talked a little bit about the way our team had begun working in Mannwa. We hadn't yet explained our intentions. It was past time, he said, for us to let them all know what we were planning to do. I then explained the program, talking especially about what we'd be able to do for their neighbors who qualify, and appealed to them for help.

"Sammuel is from the north. He didn't grow up anywhere near here. I don't even need to say that about myself. We're strangers. We know you have neighbors who need our help, but they don't trust us. You're the ones they trust. We need you to help us convince them to join this program. It's for their own good. And it could be for your good, too. Think of all the folks that come to you now and again because they need a few gourds and they don't know where to turn. Wouldn't you rather see them managing their problems without your help?"

One of the men was honest enough to say that he was against what we were doing. "*Mwen pa dakò ak sa n ap fè a.*" If we succeeded, he explained, he wouldn't be able to count on getting the cheap labor he needed to farm his land. "*Kilès ki pral travay nan jaden m?*" Others said they would speak to the families they knew best. The meeting wasn't a big success. Sammuel and I headed down the hill and back to our base in Saut d'Eau, wondering whether it had been worth the trouble.

Our program begins with a six-day training. We teach new members about the two businesses they've chosen to establish. The session we organized for the women from Mannwa was at Kafou Jòj. It was centrally located, equally inconvenient for the women of Mannwa and Boukankola on one side, and for those from Mòn Dega and Balandri on the other, and the road leading to it was good enough that our pickup truck could deliver the supplies we'd need.

But after two days, we saw that six of the women from Mannwa had failed to show up. Absences on the first day are common, but they are rare after that. Word gets around that we provide two hot meals and a cash stipend. If a woman doesn't come, you can generally assume that either she's been talked out of joining the program or that she has a serious problem.

So Sammuel and I hiked up the hill yet again to try to talk with them. We wanted to see what was keeping them away. We spoke to most of the women individually and heard a range of stories.

I had started driving a motorcycle by then, but there was just one available for the two of us that day. So Sammuel drove, and I rode behind him. We left the motorcycle in someone's front yard when we had gotten as far as we'd be able to go. Sammuel had burned out the clutch as he fought through the mud. So we called our mechanic to come fix it while we were hiking around. Then we took off up the hill. Sammuel is an athlete, an amateur soccer player in Cap Haitien, where he was born and raised. I felt as though I was chasing him, constantly trying to catch my breath.

We went to see Rose Marthe first because her home was the farthest away. When we got there, it was easy to see why she hadn't come. She had given birth only days before the session began, and couldn't make the hike up to the ridge from Wòch Djèp and then back down the other side. She wasn't yet ready even to take her infant son out of her hut. I sat on the ground outside her doorway, talking to her where she was lying with her baby on a straw mat inside. She told us that on the workshop's first day, she had sent Tinwa, a younger sister she had taken into her home. But the case managers had sent the girl home.

Sammuel had been there, so he was able to explain. Tinwa had been too shy and confused to know what to do when she got to Kafou Jòj. She couldn't say who she was or why she had come. The case managers had turned her away, not quite understanding why she was there. When we told Rose Marthe that her sister seemed too young for the training, she agreed to send her husband, Sepavre, for the next three days, and their problem was solved.

Then we headed back up toward the Mannwa ridge. We crossed over onto the small plateau, where the patches of farmland were green and full of promise. Harvest was just around the corner. We turned down the north side of the ridge, into a little valley. That's where we found Sorène. She was sitting in her yard with her little girls.

Sorène is a short woman, in her late twenties. Her mother, Manie, still has Sorène's youngest brother, Jacquesonne, at home. Manie had decided to join the program, and had been attending the workshop. But Sorène hadn't come.

She doesn't look much like Manie, except for the light brown color of their skin and their perpetually squinting eyes. Manie's narrow face contrasts sharply with her daughter's broad, high cheekbones.

The house Sorène was sharing with her partner, Princius, was on the inside edge of a small flat *lakou*. The *lakou* had been cut into the brown soil that the grassy slope was made of. It was hidden behind a field of millet. We stepped along a twisting path that led through the high millet, and then hopped down onto the shelf of flat land that the half-constructed house was sitting on. The back of the hut's frame was partially covered by a *tach* roof and was enclosed by walls of woven sticks. The front of the house was just a frame.

Sorène was sitting on a small bench with her baby on her lap. Her older girls were playing with their mother's one cast aluminum pot near three blackened cooking rocks. Nothing else was happening near the stove.

It was an awkward moment. She hadn't thought that we would return to look for her, but she knew that we had expected her at Kafou Jòj. She also knew she needed help. Her children depended on their father's farming. They had no other support. Sorène had not been able to plant crops of her own because of her baby, she owned no livestock and had no small business. And support from Princius was irregular because he was married to a second, wealthier woman, who would get most of his harvest.

"*Bonjou*, Sorène," Sammuel said.

"*Bonjou*."

"We thought you would come to the workshop."

"I can't. I can't join. Princius won't let me."

She was caught. Princius had told her that he didn't want her in the program, and she didn't know what else she could do but let him have his way.

We knew that it would be useless to try to change her mind. We asked for Princius. He was the problem. But he wasn't there, and Sorène couldn't say when he'd be back. He might come later in the day to bring his girls something to eat, but he might just stay with his wife. So we told her we were sorry, and asked her to let us know if anything changed. Then we went our way.

We left Sorène's *lakou*. We had a couple of other women to find on the north side of Mannwa, but then we hiked back up to the top of the ridge and started down the front side, looking for Micheline. She was an 18-year-old mother, living with her older sister. The sister had been her guardian since their mother's death about a dozen years before. She was selected for the program because she had nothing. Her baby's father had abandoned her before the child was even born.

On the day that I had first gone by to talk to her about joining the program, I had been to her house three times. She was alone there, and had hidden from me twice. As I walked away the second time, a guy sitting in front of a nearby house called me over. When I explained that I needed to talk to Micheline, he sent me on a wild goose chase. He explained, falsely, that she was probably at another sister's home, and he described how I could find the house by following a narrow path up the hill. While I was climbing, he got Micheline to his house. Then he called me back down the hill to join them. She was willing to talk to me, but only in the presence of a trusted adult. Her older sister wasn't around.

We sat in chairs that her neighbor offered us. He stood behind her, watching and listening. Talking to me in his presence, Micheline quickly agreed to join the program. Her neighbor encouraged her. But she was shy, almost silent. She didn't want to look at me, and I couldn't get her to say more than *"wi"* and *"non."* He was the one who got her to say that she'd come to our training.

I looked for her name on the attendance sheets from the training's first days. It was easy to find. We print the names onto a form. But beside Micheline's name there was neither a signature nor a thumbprint. About a hundred women had been attending, but she wasn't one of them. It turned out that she hadn't come because someone had convinced her sister that our program had a hidden agenda. She had heard that we would keep our own key to the house we would help Micheline build and that the animals we'd provide would turn into a curse in some way.

When Sammuel and I returned to their home, we spoke mainly with the sister. Sammuel did most of the talking.

"You can't believe what people tell you. They're just jealous because we didn't choose them."

"Really?"

"And you know that Micheline needs help. Do you want her to depend on you for the rest of her life?"

It was a long conversation, and when we headed back up to the ridge toward the main path that would lead back down to our motorcycle, we thought that we had finally won her over. She said that she'd send Micheline the next day.

But it never happened. She wouldn't let Micheline join us, though hardly anyone I met needed us more than she did.

Eventually, Micheline asked to join the program, but that was much later, long after we could have integrated her into it, after she and her sister had seen our work with other women around Mannwa.

There is little hope that we'll ever be able to help her because we are finished in her part of Boucan Carré. She just lives too far from anywhere we'll ever have a team.

Families who refuse the program once generally lose the only chance we can offer them. And it's a big loss. They're unlikely to come across other ways to remove themselves from extreme poverty.

I had a very hard time getting over Micheline's refusal. I continued to visit her regularly, holding her place open, long after we should have given it to someone else. I just couldn't resign myself to her missing the opportunity. It was difficult for me to imagine what other hope there was for her and her child. Because we failed to convince her, she remained stuck in her sister's home. And that sister was hardly well off herself.

The baby Micheline was caring for was already her second. We never found out what had happened to the first. And Micheline may be doomed to accumulate more and more children as she searches for a man willing to support her and hers. Her poverty may thus only deepen. And it was already pretty deep.

PART II:

REGULAR DAYS IN THE FIELD

Bourik chaje pa kanpe.
(A donkey with a load doesn't
stop on the way.)

Pascal and Julienne

⇒ 7 ⇐

Pascal and Louisimène

The streets of Port au Prince are filled with dust, mud, litter, garbage, filthy water, and also of shoeshiners. Every morning, roads are lined with children in school uniforms, always clean and ironed. Young men in Haiti may have to wear the same pair of sneakers regularly, but they wash them meticulously by hand, taking the time to remove the laces and wash them, too. Sunday mornings in rural Haiti are a parade of very poor people with beautifully laundered and sharply pressed clothes, their cheap shoes or sneakers shimmeringly clean. Hairstyles among Haitian women are artfully complex, and men's hair is generally painstakingly trimmed and brushed.

In Haiti, personal appearance matters. But on the days our case managers go into the field, they spend their time charging through mud and water on motorcycles. They sit in the dust as they meet with the women we serve. They just can't worry very much about how they're dressed.

Except for Pascal. Though he's just as stuck with the dirty part of the job as everyone else on our staff is, he never looks the part. His clothes are spotless and ironed. His shirt is always tucked in neatly. His sneakers are clean, or his shoes or boots are shined. One key to Pascal's success has been his discipline, and he wears that discipline with his clothes and the polished mirror-shades that usually hide his eyes.

I first met him in early 2005. He was already a Fonkoze veteran by then. He had put himself through high school as a security guard, and then had earned a promotion to a position as credit agent. He was famously successful in that second job, and he used his increased earnings to send himself to college. He then became one of the original six case managers who were hired to shepherd the first women though our pilot. He had been working as a case manager for *Chemen Lavi Miyò* for more than three years by the time I joined the team.

The job of a case manager means spending most days just visiting the families one is assigned to, moving around on foot and on motorcycle. These visits are the heart of the program, because our members will fail, despite all the assets and training we give them, despite the home repair and health interventions and other things we do, unless we accompany them very closely.

Pascal acquired a nickname on our team even before I joined it. They called him "GCM." It stands for *"gwo chimè,"* and means "big thug." His goal was never to coexist peacefully with anyone. It was to help families out of extreme poverty, and he didn't worry too much about ruffling feathers along the way. He's as kind, polite and friendly a person as you might meet most of the time, but you do not want to get in his way.

Shortly after I joined the program, I asked him if we could spend a day together. I would be supervising case managers, so I wanted to see how an excellent one did his work. He was happy to bring me around with him.

One of the first women Pascal visited was Julienne. He pulled his motorcycle all the way into her *lakou*, and parked it in the shade of a large almond tree. He sat backwards on the motorcycle's saddle, leaning back on the handlebars. Julienne sat facing Pascal on a new wooden chair.

We had originally given Julienne three goats and 1,500 gourds worth of merchandise to get started. By the day I saw her, she had accumulated five goats, a cow, a pig, and had about 3,500 gourds invested in her business.

But going over her assets with her meant actually verifying the merchandise and cash she had on hand. Pascal takes no one's word for anything. She had arranged her merchandise neatly before him, and handed him her cash to count. When he added it all up, he discovered she was short. She had less money in the business than the sales she reported had led Pascal to expect.

So he started asking questions.

He learned that she had been selling on credit. Of the 3,500 gourds in her business, over 1,300 were in her customers' hands.

Even if they were going to pay her eventually, they were reducing her capacity to continually roll her investment over. With limited capital to invest, her sales would be restricted by the number of times she could buy merchandise with the same pile of money. And she would not be able to feed her family if her income were to drop too low.

And that was a best-case scenario. People could always fail to pay her at all.

So she and Pascal talked about why she was selling on credit and why she probably wouldn't be able to eliminate the practice entirely. Women like Julienne who sell basic foodstuffs out of their homes encounter requests for credit that can be very hard to deny. You can worry that refusing will mean someone's child will go hungry or that neighbors whom you refuse will bear a grudge. And repeat customers are hard to develop among the rural poor without selling on credit at least some of the time.

Julienne and Pascal decided that she would need to reduce her sales from credit. It wouldn't be easy, but she agreed to make the effort.

After he finished working with Julienne, we went to see Louisimène. She was a little behind Julienne's progress, but not dangerously so.

There was, however, a problem. Like Julienne, she was short cash that should have been in her business. It was only a few hundred gourds, but she wouldn't say at first where the money had gone. She and Pascal sat face-to-face, she on the exposed roots of the old mango tree that was shading them from the midday sun and he on a knee-high wicker chair. What had started as a cheerful little talk – she smiled broadly when Pascal and I arrived and laughed as they started to talk about her children and her livestock – turned harder and harder as they spoke. At the beginning, she looked straight at Pascal, but she was soon looking down at his feet instead, hesitating to answer his simple questions.

"You see that there's money missing, right?"

"Yes."

"Where is it?"

"It's gone."

"I know it's gone. We both see that. Where did it go?"

"I'm not sure."

"You're not sure? You keep track of your sales. You know how much you spend and how much you make. Where is it?"

"I don't know."

Pascal kept pressing. He wouldn't let go. He finally got her to explain that she had given the money to a man she was interested in. She claimed the man said he would use it to buy beans to plant. But she knew, and eventually admitted, that he had burned through the cash spending money on himself, buying rum and cigarettes and gambling.

It wasn't the first time she had given him money. He would take her money to cockfights or to the livestock market in Nan Dal, and he'd spend it drinking, smoking, or on snacks. He'd waste more playing at *bòlet*, the private lotteries that are everywhere in Haiti, or betting on cockfights.

Pascal was furious. Louisimène would never succeed unless she could learn to hold on to her money, but she couldn't keep herself from letting a prodigal man waste it. She's a bright, capable young woman, who had begun to develop the resources and sense of ini-tiative that would draw potential partners to her, but she was so lacking in self-confidence that she felt driven to buy a scoundrel's affection with little gifts of cash. Pascal would eventually have to find the man and talk to him, but he needed to work primarily through his relationship with Louisimène.

So he did something that shocked me.

He took the cash that was in her business, counted it out carefully in front of her, tied it up in a bundle with a string, and put it in his backpack. "I'll give you back your money when you can show you understand that you're better off with money than without it."

I was stunned.

I knew I could trust Pascal with the money. It didn't occur to me that he might be stealing it.

But the money was hers. And he just took it.

I understood that he had to find a way to get her to protect her money, but I couldn't imagine that bullying her was the answer. He seemed to be replacing one abuse with another.

Pascal took my breath away. Louisimène was not a child, and yet he was confiscating money that belonged to her on nothing but his own authority. He really was a thug.

I thought about intervening, but I had no idea how. Pascal had to do something. And Louisimène reacted as though she was facing a harsh but reasonable sanction. She didn't protest, but simply lowered her head like a punished child. I watched in silence, trying to figure out my own thoughts.

Our case managers have only 30 minutes to meet with each member because they must see 50 of them every week. There's always a lot to accomplish in the half hour. They need to talk with members about their investments, but also about their family's health, their children's education – about all aspects of their lives.

And they need to go farther than mere talk. It would not be enough to just speak to members, not even if one knew how to speak very clearly. Despite his singsongy, north Haitian twang, few people can speak more clearly than Pascal. The women we work with need to dramatically change their lives. They need to change who they are. The magnitude of that challenge can lead case managers to extreme measures.

Louisimène would get her money back. But the means that Pascal had used in his effort to get her to take responsibility for it was bound to leave her wondering whether it was really hers. The only guarantee she had at that moment was whatever trust she felt for Pascal. I had to admit, at least to myself, that I would not have the strength, the audacity, to do what Pascal had done.

≥ 8 ≤

The Turkey's not the Problem

Much of the training I received focused on home visits. They are supposed to follow a clear pattern. We use a checklist, and ask our case managers to stick to it. They greet the member, ask about her family's health, check her livestock, and make sure she's following our rules for preventing cholera. They work on handwriting, and then go through seven more steps that end with a "thank you." I had begun to imagine the work as a routine: you visit each family, and just go through the procedure.

My day in the field with Pascal changed everything. Our training had sensibly focused on typical problems, but seeing Pascal work with Louisimène showed how daunting a typical problem might be. Louisimène was not the first woman to have to deal with a guy who was getting in her way. It was the sort of thing we'd be certain to come across all the time. But as I sat across from the two of them, following their exchange, I realized that I had no idea what I would have said or done in Pascal's place. I was only observing, not working, so my uncertainty didn't matter. But I had been hired to be a supervisor. I was supposed to give case managers advice about difficult situations. And I had to wonder how likely I was to know what to tell them.

I had been living in Haiti for five years, and had been visiting the country regularly for longer than that. But the more I hiked around with our team, into the deep crevices of rural Haiti that we would be working in, the more I felt my foreignness.

And it wasn't just about the children and adults who'd yell, "*Blan! Blan! Blan!*"

Nor was it about the other children who would run away crying when they saw me, frightened at the sight. I had learned to approach rural children with care, ever since the time a group of adults in the mountains above Marigot threatened me with machetes, thinking that I had been chasing their kids.

I had been in Haiti too long for such reactions to make much of an impression on me. Most of the time, I barely notice when people yell "*Blan*" at me. And for every child in the countryside who runs away, there are others who address me as "*Tonton*" or "Uncle," a sign that they see me less as a foreigner than as an older man.

What made me feel foreign were the countless details of rural Haitians' daily lives that were far removed from the life I had always lived. From the way the poorer children sleep, scattered bedless on straw mats across the uneven packed dirt floors of their parents' huts, to the way they eat, catch-as-catch-can once the food is ready rather than seated together as a family, to the tendency to explain events with mystical forces, to the pervasive evangelical Christianity, to the obsession with titles and well-shined shoes.

I had spent much of my 20s and 30s in classrooms, offices and cafes. The men I encountered through my work in Haiti spent their days farming, in their own fields or in their neighbors'. When they weren't farming, they were hanging out at *palan*, or livestock markets, looking at the animals for sale or playing dominoes or cards somewhere in the shade. I had grown up with a dog who spent her nights on my bed or my siblings'. The rural men I worked with lived around pigs, goats, cows, and poultry. Their own dogs were the nameless, scrawny, interchangeable little creatures that guarded their *lakou*, four-legged burglar alarms. I rarely passed a quiet moment without a novel in my hands. The rural Haitian adults I had come to know – even the many literate ones – rarely had a book in their hands other than the Bible, a hymnal, or the textbooks used in schools.

And nothing was more foreign to me than the simplest fact of their poverty, the hunger many rural Haitians deal with every day. The uncertainty surrounding not just the what of the next meal and the when, but even the whether. The experience of lacking even the dollar you'd need for a small, inadequate meal. Or of eating the same thing, day after day after day, because it is all you have.

These were things I'd never known.

As I stepped into my new role, and we began our first rounds of weekly visits with new members, I had to wonder whether I would be able to navigate the territory, whether my instincts would serve me or anyone else. I was enjoying the hiking and the country-side, and I felt committed to our mission. But could I contribute to our work?

Early in February 2011, I hiked up to Zaboka with Martinière. I wanted to spend a couple of days with him and the other case managers there to see how well their work had started.

We rode our motorcycles up from Kafou Jòj to Upper Viyèt and left them there, then hiked up to the entrance to the waterfall on the far side of Boukankola. We forded the small river. It was the dry season, so the cold mountain water didn't even reach our knees. We climbed up the path that follows along the water as it flows through the narrow pass, and when we got to the other side we turned up toward Gwo Monte.

"*Gwo monte*" means "big climb," and it's a good name for the area. The narrow, crooked path winds steeply up the hill. It hadn't rained since November, so the path was covered with a mixture of powdery dust and loose, hard granules of dirt. Footing was treacherous, and I fell more than once.

When we got to the top of the hill, we sat under a mango tree to make a couple of phone calls. It would be the last phone signal we would get until Wednesday, when we would hike back down. Then we worked our way down the backside of Gwo Monte, into the valley that leads to Zaboka, and waded up through the wet sand of the shallow stream until we got to the village.

We saw a few people on Sunday afternoon, but we mainly hung around in the *lakou* behind Nava's house to rest. Toward evening we walked over to the frigid spring, reduced to a dribble by months without rain, to bathe.

Martinière and I spent Monday together. He wanted my advice about Léonie, a member in Chipen, the farthest corner of our territory, a full two hours from Zaboka. But we went to see Licia first. She lives at the very top of the Chipen slope, farther from our base in Zaboka than anyone else we work with. We would hike all the way up to her house, then see Léonie and the others as we worked our way back to Zaboka.

When we got to Licia's house, she announced that she was leaving the program, even before she had finished her second month. Martinière asked her why, and what she said shocked me. She said that she's cursed. Her neighbors hate her and will prevent her from succeeding. Nothing, she said, can ever change her life.

By way of explanation, she told us the following story:

Every week, when she received the cash stipend that we give participants through their first six months, Licia would put some of it aside. After a few weeks, she had saved enough to buy a turkey. It would be a big investment, but it could pay off handsomely. Licia took her son to the market at Nan Sab, in southern Ench, and bought a large female for 600 gourds, or two weeks' stipend. She had a number of errands to run in the market, so she left her skinny 13-year-old to keep an eye on the turkey, and went her way.

A rural market like the one in Nan Sab is a lively place. Market day is the largest weekly event. People walk there from hours away. Women mostly come to buy or sell. Wealthier merchants sit in wall-less little huts, shaded under roofs of tin, *tach*, or draped sheets. They spread their merchandise in orderly rows and piles in front of them. One merchant has a half-dozen open sacks of different grains and beans. She might have a large bucket of oil and smaller ones of margarine and tomato paste. Another displays rows of plastic and aluminum housewares, dishes, cups, forks, knives, and spoons. A third has sneakers and sandals, probably used, and a fourth has t-shirts, skirts, and pants.

Poorer women find spots to sit with a single basket of their wares, or they put them on their head and circulate through the market calling out prices and items they have to sell. Men with nothing better to do stand around, gossiping over pinches of snuff. They enter the *palan*, where they look over goats, pigs, cows, and horses while they drink rum and chat. Children run around between buyers and sellers, squeezing through narrow passages or creating passages where there are none.

A group of older boys had organized a soccer game in an unplanted field on the market's periphery. Haitian boys love soccer. They'll play if they can find a ball, and they'll play if they can't, using an empty can or plastic bottle, a rag stuffed with cloths, or a hard, unripe grapefruit.

Licia's boy was more interested in the match than in his mother's new turkey. He went off to watch and when Licia returned, the turkey was gone. She looked all over the market for it, but could find no trace. Her investment disappeared the same day she made it, even before she could get it home. She felt so discouraged by the loss that she decided to leave the program. There was no point in continuing. She was obviously cursed.

Martinière listened to her patiently. They sat facing each other on small chairs she had placed under her *lakou's* largest tree, and I sat on a large exposed rock behind them. As she spoke, his every gesture – the way he nodded now and again, his smiles, his scowls, the way he shook his head – let her know he understood.

After sharing her story, she was ready to listen, too. Martinière talked a lot. But the heart of what he said was simple: She should look at the loss as a lesson. Her boy is not mature enough to be left with such a serious responsibility. The problem was not the turkey, or even a curse. And it wasn't her neighbor's jealousy.

"You can't depend on a little boy like that. He's not old enough."

Haitians say "*se mèt kò a ki veye kò a.*" This means that a body's owner is the one who keeps an eye on it. Martinière encouraged her to realize that she herself would have to take responsibility personally for her decisions. For her to leave the program right at the first setback wouldn't solve anything. After some discussion, she relented. She would continue with us, maybe a little bit wiser for her loss.

We left her *lakou* feeling good. She had presented us with our first problem, and Martinière had solved it easily.

As we walked down toward Léonie's house, Martinière reminded me what he had told me about her.

"She says that she lives in the shack halfway down the hill, but I've heard that she actually lives in Nan Sab, over in Hinche. They tell me she only comes here to collect her stipend. And I almost never see her baby. I saw him once, it's true, but all the other times she's said that he's over at her mother's, in Hinche. I don't believe her."

When we got to Léonie's house, she was waiting for us, holding her baby in her arms. If they hadn't been standing there, I would have assumed that the shack was abandoned. There was nothing lying around the *lakou*, no cooking implements and none of the baby rags you would normally see in a house that's home to an infant.

Léonie and Martinière began to talk. As they did, the baby began to cry. Martinière told her that we were not convinced that she was living in the shack with the child. I added that the *lakou* didn't look as though it had an infant living in it. "Where are the baby's clothes?"

The more we talked, the more the baby cried. Léonie drew the baby closer, but the crying continued. Martinière suggested that Léonie trying nursing, but the baby wouldn't take her breast. We heard a woman call to us from a *lakou* slightly farther down the hill. She was asking what was wrong. The baby turned, bright-eyed, toward the sound of the woman's voice. Then the woman strolled up to join us, and we watched as the baby reached toward her with little hands.

Martinière asked to hold the child, and Léonie handed her to him. As he tried to soothe and amuse the little girl, he watched her look toward the other woman, still crying.

"Léonie," Martinière asked, "is this your baby or hers?'

"She's mine."

"Really? The last time you showed me your baby, he was a little boy."

Léonie was caught in her lie. She didn't live in Chipen. She lived across the border in Hinche, where we weren't yet starting to work. She had borrowed an uninhabited shack and a baby in order to seem to qualify. I had been suspicious, but she probably could have bluffed her way through me if she had been audacious enough. She couldn't fool Martinière, though. We removed Léonie from our lists. He had already found a deserving woman on the other side of Zaboka, on the top of Gwo Monte, who needed us more. That very week, he started working with her in Léonie's place.

A view of the Mannwa ridge from the north

⇒ 9 ⇐

Manie's Goat

The first thing Manie said when we sat down was that she had something to confess. One of her goats had gotten itself twisted in its own rope. It panicked until the rope cut into its leg, leaving an ugly wound.

At the end of January, she had moved up to the top of the Mannwa ridge with Jacquesonne. They were now living in a house belonging to a cousin, within a few hundred yards of Edrès's home. So Manie had run to find him. He had gone right back with her and dressed the wound, but it hadn't yet healed completely. She was following his instructions, treating the wound with ashes from her cooking fire, and was optimistic. But she was upset at what she felt was her own negligence, and worried about what Martinière would say.

She's an older widow with four children. Only Jacquesonne still depends on her. She had nothing when she joined our program. No land, no goats. Not even a chicken. She had been living in a house that had once belonged to her, but she had been forced to sell it off to pay for her husband's funeral. The family that bought it from her had initially allowed her to stay. They were less interested in the deteriorating two-room shack than the little bit of farmable land that surrounded it. They started to plant crops, but they had no need to drive her out of what had once been her home. She got by on handouts and on what Jacquesonne could earn in their neighbors' fields. But when the home's buyer saw her in the program, he started pressuring her to leave, jealous because we hadn't taken his family as well. Manie had a cousin who had abandoned a house in Mannwa to live in downtown Mirebalais with her children, and Manie got permission for herself and Jacquesonne to share its one room. At least until they could build the home that we would help them with. Her daughter Sorène joined them with her little girls shortly after that.

Manie owned no furniture. So we sat on the ground in a shady spot out front, and talked.

I was filling in for Martinière. Normally, he would see Manie every Wednesday morning. He and the rest of the team would leave the base in Zaboka by 6:00 AM, hike up out of Deniza and down the Gwo Monte path that leads back to the waterfall. The three other guys would continue to follow the path down along the waterfall to spend the day working in Boukankola and Dimèren, but Martinière would cross the stream and then hike up the back of Wòch Djèp to get to Rose Marthe's house.

I had started my day at our office in Saut d'Eau, instead. So I left my motorcycle in Viyèt and hiked up to Mannwa from the south. The shadeless path winds upward through rocky bean fields with a broad view of lower Boucan Carré. When I got to the top of the ridge, I walked past the church and onto the thickly planted plateau behind it. I stopped at Manie's house on my way to Wòch Djèp. She was my first visit of the day.

She's a small woman with light brown skin and short, graying hair that she keeps combed tightly along her scalp. Her soft, high voice is clear, but always sounds a little weary. She doesn't speak. She sighs. We talked first about her goats because that was what was on her mind. She knows that she needs to keep them tied up. If one of them gets into someone's garden they could decide just to kill it. Even if the garden's owners are kind, they'll confiscate the goat until Manie pays damages that she can't afford. So she's conscientious about keeping the goats tied. But if you tie them, you need to keep an eye on them, because they can get excited and panic and then do themselves harm, as Manie's had done. She promised me that she and Jacquesonne would pay closer attention to them.

The other thing we talked about was her *sòl*.

A *sòl* is a savings club, very common in Haiti. Martinière organized one for members in and around Mannwa. Each week ten of them give him 100 gourds from the 300-gourd stipend that we provide for the first six months of the program, and Martinière gives one of the women 1,000 gourds. As a woman's turn to collect the pot approaches, she talks with Martinière about the best ways to invest the money. It's a good way to teach the women to plan.

But on Martinière's previous visit, he had distributed two weeks' worth of stipends to each member because he hadn't seen them the previous week. They therefore paid two weeks' worth of contribution to their *sòl* and two different women had collected the pot. Manie had gone along with it, because Martinière told her to. But she hadn't understood why. So when I gave her 300 gourds, and asked her to give me back her *sòl* contribution, she tried to give me 200 gourds. She insisted that Martinière had taken that much the previous week. I refused to take more than 100, but I couldn't explain why Martinière had taken more. I wasn't sure what he had done. Manie simply accepted my decision just as she had accepted the fact that Martinière had taken twice as much.

From Manie's house, I had a long walk down the hill to get to Rose Marthe, my second visit of the day. After spending her first weeks with her new baby, staying very close to home, she was starting to get around. She hadn't yet recovered fully from childbirth, but she was able to leave her shack and do most of her chores. She was putting her weekly stipend to good use. There was a full pot, boiling as it sat on her three rocks, with a scrap-wood fire beneath it. She told me that she and her kids had been eating every day.

She had also bought two small chairs since she entered the program, and we sat in the shade under a tree near the entrance to her *lakou* as we talked. The yard had been thoroughly swept. Martinière's messages about cleanliness and hygiene were sinking in. As we sat and chatted, we watched her neighbor's turkeys strutting noisily on the hill in front of us.

It was Rose Marthe's turn to receive the *sòl*, so she and I spent most of our time talking about how she wanted to invest it. She is the one who explained to me why Martinière had taken 200 gourds from Manie the previous week, so I asked her to explain the matter to Manie the next time they met, and she said that she would.

When I asked her what she planned to do with the *sòl*, she told me she wanted to buy another goat. She had the two goats we had given her already, but wanted a third. She likes taking care of the animals, and doesn't feel pressed to make money more quickly. It's harvest time and for the moment, her family has enough food coming in from the fields to keep them fed. So we agreed that she would go ahead, and I added that she should make sure to have the goat nearby for Martinière's next visit. He would want to confirm that she had used her money as she said she would, but he would also want to vaccinate it.

After hiking all the way west to Wòch Djèp, I turned back to the east and continued down the slope toward Lalyann.

The path across Lalyann snakes up and down a series of smaller ridges that spike northward from the main east-west one. The path is narrow, and the thick grass can make it hard to see whether I'm putting my foot down on it or beside it. I slip in a couple of places, and fall two or three feet. But I remember that Martinière does this walk every week, and I just keep walking. I spend some time talking to Magalie, and then I continue to Omène's house.

She lives with her husband Elga and their children in a home in her in-laws' *lakou*. Elga comes and goes. He sometimes leaves for weeks at a time when he can find agricultural work in the rice fields of Ponsonde or the cane fields near Lascahobas. When he's not home, his parents are nasty to Omène. They treat her as though she was a child who they can boss around and even punish. When she told them that she would like to go and spend a few days visiting her own parents, they forbade it, threatening to beat her if she disobeyed.

Elga and Omène

It was the last straw. Martinière had heard this from her before. She had explained to him that she needed to move out of the house to get beyond their reach. He had asked her to have Elga there for his next visit. He wanted to hear the husband's side of things. Martinière would take Omène's side come what may. That's his job. But the problem would be very different depending on whether Elga sided with her or with his parents. Martinière wanted to make sure he had the full picture.

Elga was waiting with Omène when I got there, and I found out that he's on her side —100%. He's ashamed of the way his parents treat his wife, and anxious to get her into a new house as quickly as possible. He had already cleared a piece of land in the corner of a small field that he farms, and collected the materials he'll need for construction. He led me down to it and showed me the piles of rocks, sand, support poles, and *tach*. I asked him and Omène to be sure to coordinate the move with Martinière. That will help ensure that Omène continues to receive our support in her new home. And Martinière will be providing construction materials – a little cement and some tin roofing – that will make their small house more solid than it could otherwise be. He'll even be able to pay a builder, or pay Elga directly if he's able to do the work himself.

From Omène's house, I descend farther across Lalyann down into the valley. I turn northward along one small ridge that stretches downward out to Chrismène's house. After meeting with Chrismène, I make the long hike straight back up to Mannwa.

As I reach the northernmost corner of the central part of the ridge I find Marie Paul. She's the last member I see on the way out of Mannwa. Marie is doing well in some ways. She's been managing her subsistence allowance carefully, and has already been able to buy several animals beyond the ones we gave her.

But when I arrived at her home at about 2:00, she hadn't made food yet that day. She was waiting for her stipend so she could go to the market. She wouldn't prepare a meal until early evening. One of her older boys was getting ready to grill some hard kernels of dried corn over a small fire just to ward off the hunger pangs. Imagine a meal of the unpopped kernels left over after someone makes popcorn.

Marie feels so much pressure to build up her assets that she is using money that could feed her children right now to plan for a better future instead. It's admirable, but it leaves her children suffering needlessly in the short term. We are in a hurry to see her make progress, just as she's in a hurry to move forward, because we all know that 18 months is not a lot of time to change her life. But 18 months is still 18 months, not 18 days. If we can convince her to trust the process, she could spend a little more money now to improve her children's lives right away. That's something for her to talk about with Martinière.

As I walked down from Gapi back to my motorcycle in Viyèt, it started to rain. That was a bad sign. I hadn't had a chance to eat in the morning before I left, and I had been hiking up and down the slopes around Mannwa for hours. I was tired. As the topsoil that covered the road out of Viyèt began to turn into mud, the one thing I would need would be the strength to keep my motorcycle's wheels straight against their desire to slip one way or the other. I had fallen a couple of times before I made it even a quarter of the way.

And it was starting to get dark.

As the road grew more slippery, mud collected around the back wheel. With each new fall, I'd need time to take a stick and dig some of the mud out again.

Viyèt is full of families we work with, and I was soon surrounded by men and women I knew. A couple of the husbands tried to hold onto and guide the motorcycle as I picked my way through especially slippery spots, but the work got harder and harder for all of us. My feet were so covered with mud that I was slipping as much as the motorcycle was.

Itane eventually convinced me to give up the fight. I left the motorcycle with her, and hired a professional taxi driver to take me back to Mirebalais.

From Mirebalais, it would be easy to get a ride to Saut d'Eau. In fact, long before the driver made it to Mirebalais with me, Martinière had telephoned, worried because I hadn't gotten back. I gave him a short version of my story, and he left Saut d'Eau right away. He was waiting to pick me up in Mirebalais, and he drove me back to Saut d'Eau.

Two days later, I returned to Viyèt to retrieve the motorcycle, and I could see the basketball-sized lump of mud Itane had removed from around its rear axel. She had washed the motorcycle with care.

⇒ 10 ⇐

Mòn Dega

My one and only uncle, whom I loved dearly, was a doctor, a wounded World War II veteran who became a pioneer in rehabilitative medicine. He spent a long career treating cases of paralysis, and taught our family to fear motorcycles and trampolines. The spinal injury ward he ran at Boston University's hospital was full of motorcycle accident victims.

But our work requires a motorcycle. In many of the areas we go, it is the best way, the only really practical way, to get around. So I started riding a few weeks after joining the team. It wasn't long before I took my first fall.

The front wheel slipped as I pulled out of a riverbed in Saut d'Eau. In my panic, I continued to hang on, giving it gas, and the motorcycle dragged me across the gravelly road. I got scraped up a bit. I was with Bonissant at the time, one of the experienced case managers, and he put both hands on his head in the standard Haitian gesture of dismayed surprise. I was dizzy. I wasn't going to be getting back on my motorcycle, or even on the back of his. So we called one of our drivers, and he came with a truck and gave me a ride back to Saut d'Eau. I spent the afternoon feeling woozy, throwing up every now and again.

But my wounds wouldn't have been much to worry about if they hadn't gotten infected. First my shoulder, then my foot, swelled up, and I was out of the field for more than a month.

When I was ready to start work again, the team assigned me my own motorcycle. Gauthier thought that I would have an easier time if I had just one bike to get used to. Until then, I was used to grabbing hold of any motorcycle that was available, just as many of my colleagues would.

The bike Gauthier assigned to me was a Chinese dirt bike, made by a company called "Lifan." It's a tall bike with a black seat and gas tank and cheap plastic cutouts in royal blue and white along its sides. The white cutouts below the saddle are marked "Cool Boy," for some reason. That could have become a joke except that the name "lifan" is already funny enough.

I looked up the words in Chinese, and "li" means "power." "Fan" means a sail. I'm not sure what they would mean together, but a Chinese brand name may not need to make more than a moderate amount of sense.

In Creole, however, the meaning is clear. "*Li fann*" means either "it splits" or "it is split," and we would sometimes say that my motorcycle cuts through the road or the mud or the rivers I had to ford. But we would also say that it was splitting Steven in two. I would fall a lot. I did not pick up the skill very quickly.

So the first time I had to ride up Mòn Dega, I was not excited. In Haitian Creole, "*dega*" means "disaster" or "mess." The name "*Mòn Dega*," or "Disaster Mountain," suits the road that winds up from Domon to Nan Mango. It's a steep and narrow series of sharp turns. Its surface alternates between large, fixed rocks and loose gravel, each of which presents a challenge. The larger rocks can catch and twist your front tire, sending you crashing to the ground if you don't react to them quickly and correctly. The gravel can have you stalling out as it slides out from under your rear wheel while you try to climb the trail's steeper stretches.

The four male case managers on my team all had families they worked with in various neighborhoods on the mountain. But many of the families that Orweeth, Bonissant and Ellien worked with lived only part of the way up. So Orweeth and Ellien would usually leave their motorcycles at the bottom and hike the rest of the way. It just seemed easier. Bonissant was experienced enough as a driver that it didn't much matter to him.

The three of them encouraged me to leave my cycle at the bottom of the hill as well. The road was too difficult, they said, for a novice. Ellien and Orweeth especially told me that I couldn't do it.

But Martinière had to ride all the way up to Nan Mango and beyond to meet with his families. It would be too much ground to cover easily on foot. And he wasn't inclined to fear the road himself or to coddle me by indulging any fear I might have. So he just said, "Let's go," and I decided to give it a try.

Getting to the base of the first hill was easy enough. You turn off the main highway in Domon onto the Boucan Carré road. After fording the Boucan Carré River, you turn slightly to the north, rather than following the curving main road toward Difayi and Chanbo. Once you cross the river, the ride to the base of the mountain may be rocky in places and a little bit muddy in others, but it rises slowly, snaking upward comfortably to a public water source, where children assemble with their gallons and buckets to haul the water their families need every day.

Few Haitian families have running water at home. Members have to go to whatever source their community might have with buckets and jugs to get the water a household needs and carry it home. In some regions, it can become a day's principal occupation, especially during the dry season. I've worked in parts of Lagonav where people have to walk three or four hours each way during the worst parts of the year.

The people who live near the base of Mòn Dega are luckier. Their water source is a concrete box that acts as a cistern, collecting water from a spring that's been capped higher up the hill. The cistern has a couple of faucets in its base. Women bring their laundry close and spend the day washing it and sharing their gossip on the grassy lawn that spreads below. Young people hang around playing and joking. Some sit right on the cistern, others gather in small groups on the grass.

It's great that they have access to good water, but it means that you take the first steep slope on a motorcycle in front of a crowd of curious witnesses.

I stopped near the water source to watch how Martinière took the hill. He followed a narrow line that ran up the far right side of the road, where other motorcycles had cleared away some of the loose rocks. He had been accelerating as he hit the bottom of the slope, so he was most of the way up before he dropped into first gear. As he did, he followed the thin bare path as it crossed from right to left, and then he turned up around the corner to the right toward the next hill.

I braced myself, slipped into first gear, and then hit the gas. I tried to do as Martinière had done, but when I got to the spot where the narrow path crossed the road, I went slightly off of it and onto the rocks. My front tire hit one that was fixed into the dirt beneath it, and jerked to the left. I fell backward, and the motorcycle fell on top of me. Before I knew it, I was lying on the ground with my left leg pinned underneath my motorcycle. The left rearview mirror and left rear turn signal were in pieces, but things were otherwise OK.

The kids at the water source were laughing and pointing, but two of the older boys could see that the way I was lying, with my head downhill from my feet and my leg pinned underneath the bike, I would have a hard time extricating myself on my own. So they ran to me and stood the motorcycle up. The only place I was bruised was in my ego, but it would be challenging to start up the hill again by myself because the motorcycle would have to be in neutral to start, and putting it into neutral risked sending me rolling backward down the hill. So one of the boys held the back of the motorcycle in place, and I started off again. Martinière was waiting at the top of the next hill, and we continued on our way.

The long third hill curves steeply around to the right. It's covered with gravel, except for a thin, bare strip along its far right side, right up against the solid rock slope that the road was cut into. Martinière once again accelerated as he hit the bottom of the slope. He worked his clutch nimbly to shift into first at just the right moment and gave his motor relief when it sounded as though it might stall. So he got to the top without difficulty.

I had two problems. On one hand, I am not nimble with my clutch. On the other, I lack the confidence to accelerate over the loose rocks that litter the base of the hill.

So I was already in first gear when I started up the hill, and I had too little momentum to make it easily to the top. Instead of using my clutch skillfully, I have taught myself to do the next best thing. As soon as I sense that the motor's starting to fail, I put my two feet on the ground and start helping out, like a skinny Fred Flintstone driving a dirt bike. The technique gets me out of a lot of trouble. It helps with mud and water and lots of hills.

But it wasn't enough for this one. The motorcycle stalled. And as I was trying to turn it slightly so that it would stay in place when I put it in neutral to start it again, I lost balance and it fell over.

This time, I had been able to pull my leg away from it and let go, so I didn't fall with it. But lifting it up on the hill was a chore. It's heavy for me, and I didn't have good leverage.

I eventually got it standing, however, and started again before Martinière had the chance to turn back to help me. And by now we were approaching Plenn Dipò, the first community we would cross as we continued up the hill. This is where most of Orweeth's work would be, so I was beginning to understand why he'd rather walk.

When we got to the far side of Plenn Dipò, we reached a fork. The road on the right climbed a short hill toward Bwajoli. Ellien worked with families there. Martinière's route turned toward the left, where Mòn Blanch, the White Mountain, stood before us. It is steep and narrow. It probably got its name because it is covered, except in the middle of the rainy season, with inches of powdery, grayish-white dust. Here, the easier line is up the far left side of the hill, and I was able to get the cycle onto that line. But as much as

I worked my clutch and my two Fred-Flintstone feet, I stalled on the hill. Three times. At least I didn't fall.

Mòn Blanch is the longest and steepest in the series of hills that the road climbs up to Nan Mango and Balandri. But it's not the most difficult. The nameless hill behind it is much worse. It's neither as steep nor as long as Mòn Blanch, but the only clear path through it winds up and around a series of large rocks. The smaller rocks that surround them are loose. The large rocks mean that you have to do a lot of steering, and the small ones mean that it is easy to slip each time you do. I took two falls and I stalled once, but when we got to the top we were nearly in Nan Bento, and Martinière was clearly pleased with me.

Going downhill should be much easier. Motorcycles are heavy. If you can keep them moving forward, they do not want to fall. I had watched how good drivers, like Pascal, simply coast over rocks.

But fear makes the downhill ride challenging, too. It is easy to slip off the thin, bare tracks that wind down the rocky, gravel-strewn road, and putting your feet on the ground to stabilize yourself sometimes just makes things worse because you need your right foot to work the rear brake.

I fell twice on the way down, the second time just above the cistern near the bottom. I guess I needed to give the kids something to laugh at before I drove home.

Riding down Mòn Blanch

⇒ II ⇐

Not Copying

For five months, Celimène Desir has been trying to learn to write her name.

She is an excitable, outgoing woman, a mother of six who lives in Plenn Dipò, across a field from the base of Mòn Blanch, the steepest of the series of slopes that lead up the Mòn Dega road.

She's shown a willingness to work hard in her first months in our program. When we gave her merchandise to start a small commerce, the business took off right away. Her model was simple. She would buy sacks of charcoal at the highland markets in Nan Mango and Opyèg and then sell them in Difayi and Domon, below. It was almost foolproof. The charcoal would reliably sell for more once she got it down the hill, closer to town, even if she sold it by the sack. If she was willing to take the time to break up the sack and sit in the market, selling it in small bags, she could make even more. But the model was also very demanding. She would have to hike twice a week down the mountain with a sack of charcoal balanced on her head. And as the business began to grow, she would have to find someone else – her husband or her older son – to carry a second sack.

So she wasn't afraid of hard work.

But all that willingness hasn't enabled Celimène to learn to write her name.

We don't have the time it would take to teach literacy to the women we work with, but we want them to at least be able to sign their names. And most of them want that, too. It's a question of human dignity. They feel better about themselves when they can sign their name to a form or a list rather than leaving a thumbprint.

Most of the women we work with learn to sign fairly easily, and most of the ones who struggle have poor vision. This is especially true of the older ones. All they would really need is reading glasses, but getting them appropriate reading glasses and teaching them to use them isn't easy.

Others have trouble with the small muscle coordination they need to control the movements of their pencil or pen. They're used to the larger movements that farming, laundry, and other hard work require, but they struggle to learn to hold a pen.

Celimène could see well enough, and seemed to be able to manipulate her pencil. We weren't quite sure what her problem was.

Her case manager, Orweeth, had been trying to help her for months and they had very little to show for all the work they had done. Many women would have told their case manager that they hadn't done their homework. They'd say that their child had mistakenly run off to school with their notebook or had taken their pencil. The case manager would then have to go to a lot of trouble to get them to keep making the effort. But Celimène showed more determination – of a sort – than that. When Orweeth and I got to her house, she presented him with her well-done homework: two pages of beautifully copied little C's. Five months into the program, and she was still working on her name's first letter.

But one of her children had done the work for her, which only shows that she was frustrated enough to want an easy way out of the difficulty. When we asked her to make a C in front of us, she couldn't do it.

So I decided to sit back and watch Orweeth offer a writing lesson. He drew a line of C's across the top of a page, and asked Celimène to copy one. What she drew looked like something between a U and a V. Each time she put her pencil to the page, she would make a downward stroke, slightly curved, almost like a parenthesis. Once she got to the lowest point of the parenthesis, she would start back upward to make the other side of the U.

Again and again, she started to turn back upward and Orweeth tried to stop her. He imagined that her parenthesis was the C, and that her problem was that she was extending what looked to him to be the bottom part of the C too far, bringing the line back upward. Again and again, he told her with increasing exasperation not to bring the line back upward, not to close the C's opening. Again and again, she did the same thing. Orweeth wasn't getting anywhere, but he was getting frustrated, so I asked him to step aside.

I had been watching Celimène closely, and I thought I had made a discovery. She was seeing the C's half-moon shape clearly, and was intent on trying to reproduce it. That was, in fact, the way we had been explaining how to make a C. Simply trace a half moon. But each time she put her pencil to the page, she made her first movement downward. Once she had done so, she had no choice but to turn the line back upwards. Otherwise, the half moon would be incomplete.

So instead of telling her to stop turning the line back upwards, I asked her to change the way she was starting. I told her to start by making a line that moved back toward the left from the point where she placed the point of her pencil on the page. Having done so, I reasoned, she would be forced to turn the line back to the front, and would thus have her C.

Celimène could make no sense of my suggestion. She continued to make little U's.

So I thought again for a moment, and then decided that, rather than repeating the same instructions or giving her another explanation to follow, I would pose a problem.

I started with a question. I asked her whether she thought her C was the same as mine or different. She immediately answered that it was different, but when I asked her to explain, she merely said that mine was better.

I didn't want her to consider the more confident stroke of my pen. I wanted her to focus on the direction her C's were facing. So I tried again, asking her which way my C was pointing.

Creole has words for left and right, but rural Haitians don't always use them. They distinguish one side from the other by gesturing with their hands. So when I asked Celimène which way my C was pointing, she said "*konsa*" or "like this," and pointed toward the right. I asked her whether her C was pointing in the same direction, and she could see that it wasn't. She said hers was pointing up. I then asked her how she could make her C's point in the same direction as mine.

Now it was her turn to think.

What she then did surprised me. She started her pencil at the rear-most point of the half moon and made the top half of the C with one line. Then she returned with her pencil to the point she had started from, and made the lower half. We prepared a page for her to do as homework, and we'll see next week whether she's on the right track, but she seems to have broken through something that was getting in her way.

Whatever Celimène learned from the experience, I certainly learned more.

We had been treating Celimène as though she was a photocopier. It's the way we generally teach women in our program to write their names, and it works for almost all of them. In anything from a few weeks to a few months, they are signing. You can give them all-caps, small case, or even cursive. For most of them, it doesn't matter. They see a design in front of them, and they learn to reproduce it. One of the pleasures of management in our program is to see the weekly forms that members sign to verify receipt of their cash stipend. At the beginning, most members can leave only a thumbprint. But week by week, more of them sign. The stipends end after six months, and just a handful of thumbprints remain.

But a human being is not a machine. Celimène's work could not succeed as mindless reproduction. Until she started to grasp the essential points of the simple image we were asking her to trace, the task of making even her name's first letter was beyond her. And until we learn to take the time we need to understand what is getting in a person's way as they struggle to change their life, we will have little chance of providing the help she needs.

Elga and Chrismène

⇒ 12 ⇐

Matlòt

Chrismène lives with her children at the lower, northern edge of Lalyann, on a ridge that descends from Mannwa toward the valley between Boucan Carré and Thomonde, east of Wòch Djèp.

When we first met her, she told us that her husband, Elgué, had abandoned her to seek his fortune in the Dominican Republic. She was just 23 then, with an oldest daughter who must have been eight or nine. The girl was her second child. Her first had died in infancy. She had little to feed her children with: just two chickens and a small plot of land she would farm that stretched below her narrow *lakou*.

But Chrismène flourished from the moment she joined us. Martinière watched her with affectionate pride as her livestock grew and multiplied because of the excellent care she took of them. She invested cash that she saved from her stipend into her farming, and was rewarded with strong harvests. And she worked hard and with discipline to take advantage of the materials the program made available for her to repair her home and build a latrine.

But one thing surprised us.

Single women usually have a very hard time with home repair unless they have a father, brother or older son around to help them. There is a lot we insist that members do toward building their own homes, things more easily done with a partner's help. Chrismène is a small woman, and her children are still too young to be much help. When the program started, she didn't yet own a pack animal. She would need someone to help her do the heavier lifting. Her older sister came and stayed with her for a few days to help her lug the dirt and rocks she would need to build up the walls of her house. But getting the cement for her latrine and the tin roofing from Kafou Jòj up the slope to Mannwa, and then back down the other side to her home in the very back of Lalyann would be no joke. And with Elgué in the Dominican Republic, we weren't sure how she'd manage.

As things turned out, it was not a problem. Plentiful help came from what seemed a surprising source. The program member who lives closest to Chrismène is Omène. She and Elga had moved out of his parents' *lakou* by then, and they were living in their half-constructed new house on the same ridge that Chrismène lived on, a few hundred yards higher up toward Mannwa. She, Chrismène and Elga had explained that Elga is Elgué's twin brother.

Over and over, Elga would come to his sister-in-law's aid. He is a friendly and energetic man, and we had seen enough to like him when he found a way to take his wife's side against his parents without alienating the mother and father who raised him. So we had reason to hope he'd be kind enough to offer his abandoned sister-in-law some support.

But there seemed to be no limit to his goodwill. He helped her collect the lumber she needed to build her house, to get her heavier materials to Lalyann from Kafou Jòj, to work in her fields, and to manage her animals. Martinière made an effort to encourage him every time they met, letting him know how much we appreciated his support. He'd even give him a few hundred gourds now and again to thank him. When we'd see him during our hikes through Mannwa, Martinière always took the time to chat: a big handshake, a pat on the back, a few kind words. He'd listen to anything Elga wanted him to know about the progress he and Omène were making. And they'd talk about his sister-in-law, Chrismène, too. Elga is average height for a Haitian farmer, and he has a farmer's thin, muscular frame. Martinière dwarfed him. His big arm would engulf the smaller man's shoulders as they stood to talk.

But Elga's willingness turned out to be less surprising than we had thought.

One day, several months into the program, Martinière was passing through the neighborhood, and he went by one of the regular meetings that Edrès, who is among other things the Partners in Health extension worker for Mannwa, holds for the mothers in the area. Both Chrismène and Omène were there.

As Martinière arrived, he greeted Edrès first. Then he made a point of talking to the various women who were present. Many were from our families, and Martinière was responsible for all of them. A neighbor – a small, older man who farms land along the Mannwa ridge – came by to talk something over with Edrès. Looking at how well Chrismène and Omène seemed to be doing since they entered the program, the neighbor remarked loudly and clearly enough for all to hear that Elga's wives were looking good.

Martinière looked at the two women and they looked at him. Edrès looked from Martinière to Chrismène to Omène. None knew quite what to say. Finally, they all just laughed.

Elgué had never gone to the Dominican Republic. Elgué, Chrismène's husband, didn't exist. He and Elga were the same person, husband to both women. He had been helping not his sister-in-law, but his second wife. The three of them explained that they had been afraid to tell us the truth, worried – mistakenly – that we would accept only one of the two women into the program. So they conspired to deceive us, and they succeeded for a while. Their neighbors, the other women we work with, and even Edrès had played along with the ruse.

In French, a "*matelot*" is a sailor. The word appears to be connected to the word for mattress. Two sailors would share one hammock by sleeping at different times. They'd be bunkmates. In French, the shared sleeping arrangement turned into a name for the class of sailors themselves.

The Creole word "*matlòt*" is most likely derived from a feminine version of the French, but its meaning is different. *Matlòt* are women, like Chrismène and Omène, who share the same husband.

It's not unusual in rural Haiti. We regularly come across situations in which men have two or three wives. They may be married legally to one of them. Even without a legal marriage, however, community members may recognize one of the women as the *madanm marye*, or the real wife. But the men are not necessarily legally married to any of them, even when they have stable relations with all.

And it is not surprising that families of *matlòt* are very well represented in our program. Men who establish two or more households are bound to have more trouble supporting their wives and kids. They must spread both their harvests and whatever cash they might earn more thinly.

But Elga is committed to working hard for both women, and he shows no signs of interest in others. He lives by a simple rule to minimize conflict: "I never keep any of the money I earn. It all goes straight to Omène or to Chrismène. If I need a few gourds for a bit of snuff or a sip of rum, I have to ask one of them." He and Omène have six children together, and he has four surviving children with Chrismène. The two women both know that Omène is his principal wife, but he says he is unswerving in his commitment to Chrismène. "I could never abandon her. I've made her suffer too much."

And the two women get along well. They often walk together all the way from their homes in Lalyann to the market in Chanbo. And the first time I saw them there, they cheerfully posed for a group photo with Martinière. I wondered at the lack of evident jealousy. When I see one or the other with Elga, I feel as though I'm looking at a happy couple. He seems a loving and affectionate man with both.

But one day I was in Lalyann and I asked them to pose together with Elga. Both women were glad to take separate photos, couple by couple. But neither woman wanted to take a photo with both Elga and her *matlòt*. Omène was especially firm. So there is something about their relationship that they do not wish to share.

⇒ 13 ⇐

The Importance of Santiague

I didn't see Santiague very often during almost two years in Bay Tourib. He must be in his 70s, a short, roundish man with what always looks like a few days' growth of thin, greyish-white beard with bristles that stand out strongly against his dark face. The one sure way to find him was to drive up on a Sunday afternoon, and arrive in time to visit the *gagè*, or cockfights, held just across the stream that marks the entrance to the town.

Cockfights are popular in Haiti, especially in rural Haiti. One sees cockfighting rings everywhere. Usually, they are little more than squares made up of four benches, planks nailed onto rough wooden posts that have been driven into the earth. Knee-high walls of wooden planks in front of the benches trace the outside of the ring. Often they sit near a large tree or two that shade the ring from the late afternoon sun.

The fights start late in the day, and the space around the ring fills with men. Women rarely attend, except the ones who set up businesses. Snuff, cigarettes, rum, and fried snacks are especially popular.

Santiague was certain to be at the *gagè* in Bay Tourib every Sunday, watching the fights and drinking locally brewed rum with his friends. He's a cheerful, friendly man, and could be very effusive if one didn't see him early.

I know him mainly through his daughter, Mémé. She's about my age, and not much taller than her dad. She works as a cook and housekeeper at the residence in Bay Tourib that our team shared with the Partners in Health clinic's staff. She's also a leader in the Bay Tourib community, one of the founders of O.D.B., the Organization for the Development of Bay Tourib. That's the peasant group that originally invited Partners in Health to open a clinic in their town and then worked hard to help us get our program started there, too. As one of the most comfortably literate of the organization's founders, she serves as its secretary. People look to her. Her opinions matter. Her grandparents raised her, and they must have made a commitment to her education beyond what most other Bay Tourib parents were offering their girls at the time.

Santiague first came to my attention in August 2011, on the day we launched our program in Bay Tourib. We had spent three months selecting 350 new families, and were holding a large celebration in the Roman Catholic church, the town's largest building. More than a thousand people attended.

In all the confusion, a guest lost her camera and cell phone. They were in her bag, which she had put down for a moment. When she went back to the bag, the stuff was gone. One of my colleagues took the microphone, and explained to the crowd that someone must have accidently picked up the phone and camera. He asked that they be returned. He said that we were certain that it was a mistake and that we would not ask any questions of the person who returned them, just offer our thanks.

Nothing happened.

He repeated his announcement a couple of times over the course of 30 minutes or so. The repetitions didn't help.

When Santiague got wind of the theft, he walked up to the front of the assembled crowd and told us to give him the mike. I'm not sure why we just handed it over. We had thought ourselves to be in charge. But there was something in the way he asked. It seemed as though there was no choice. As soon as he started to talk, we were surprised to see how quickly the boisterous crowd quieted down.

"Whoever took the foreigner's stuff: If it's not brought to me by the end of the week, whatever happens to you is meant for you," he said. "*Sa k ap rive w, se pou ou li ye.*" He then added, "I'm the one who says so."

Both the camera and the phone turned up the next day.

To influence what happens in a community sometimes requires finding someone who has real clout. In Bay Tourib, Santiague has clout. He is a *gangan*, a practitioner of *vodoun*.

It's not easy to know exactly what powers his neighbors might believe Santiague to possess, but no one would be comfortable making him angry. Men and women like Santiague are often able to harm or to heal using an advanced knowledge of herbs and other medicinals. But people also believe that they know how to make use of mystical forces. Some make a lot of money with the power they are thought to have. Santiague was not making himself wealthy, but he was making a living and had earned a great deal of respect.

We thought of Santiague when we were facing a different problem. Three *matlòt*, Yveroselène, Roselène, and Dieukifaite, were being beaten by their husband, Gelik.

It's easy to imagine why Gelik would feel threatened by our program. We were giving his wives a real chance to learn to take care of their children and themselves. They might discover that they didn't need him any more. And less than two years after they graduated, two had abandoned him and the third was getting ready to leave. But at the time, they weren't yet striking out on their own, so we had to find a way to protect them.

We first tried to address the man himself, to make him understand that he had to stop his violence. When we spoke to Gelik, he told us to mind our own business.

Then we decided to go through official, legal channels. We spoke to the KASEK, an important local elected official. Since there are no police in rural areas of Haiti, KASEK are generally responsible, to some degree, for law and order. The KASEK said that he'd talk to Gelik, but either he didn't follow through or he spoke with him to no effect.

The next time we heard that Gelik had once again beaten Yveroselène, we tried to confront him with numbers. I hiked up to their home behind a hill, just a couple of hundred yards from our residence, with several of the case managers, some pretty large men. A short, skinny little man like Gelik might bully his wives, but he wasn't going to want to get mixed up heavyweights like Ricot and Anselet. But by the time we got there, he had run off.

A few days later, Gelik was hanging around outside the Bay Tourib clinic, drunk. When I spoke to him there, he swore at me rudely and boasted about how he would beat his wives whenever he wanted to. It was his right, he said, and none of our concern. It was even, he said, our fault, because since joining our program they had gotten uppity.

I went to Mémé for advice. She seemed to know everyone in Bay Tourib, and could often help us out by sharing what she knew of the complex histories behind the issues we were facing. She knew Gelik well, and didn't think we'd be able to change him. "That's just how he is." "*Se konsa li ye.*"

So I told her I had an idea. I asked her whether she thought her father would be willing to help. She hadn't thought of that. She smiled and said that she suspected that he would. Then she agreed to put Santiague in touch with me.

Phone service in a place like Bay Tourib is very limited. The only way to get a signal is to hike up one of the hills that surround the town. So few people have cell phones, and they are used only to make occasional calls to family members in nearby cities like Hinche, Thomonde and Mirebalais, or in Port au Prince.

Communication within Bay Tourib is simpler. If the person you need is likely to be within a few hundred yards, you yell. If not, either you go find the person yourself or you find someone who will be walking somewhere near where the person is likely to be.

Mémé doesn't like to hike around much herself, so she usually just sends word that she needs someone, and they appear. She's not intimidating the way her father is, but people tend to do what she asks. Santiague showed up within a couple of days, and he had already been briefed.

He came by the clinic one afternoon, and we sat in the shade on the benches that had been full in the morning with patients waiting to see the one doctor there. The mountain air grows cool quickly in the afternoon, and Santiague wore a light jacket and a heavy wool hat, though it must have been in the 60s. I had been out in the field all day, visiting families with one of the case managers. I had gulped down the cornmeal porridge that Mémé and the kitchen team had left for me, but I hadn't yet had a chance to bathe in the cold stream that runs behind the residence. I was tired and sore.

Though it wasn't Sunday, Santiague was effusive. Apparently, one could enjoy local rum even without a cockfight. I can't say how much of his reaction depended on the way Mémé explained the situation to him, but when he and I spoke, he was quick to agree that husbands shouldn't hit their wives, that it's not right. "*Sa pa fèt ankò.*" "It's not done anymore." At some time in the past it might have been the usual thing, but it's no longer OK.

I asked Santiague whether he'd talk with Gelik. "We need Gelik to change, and so we need the help of someone he really respects." We were all outsiders. Gelik had no reason to listen to us. "But he's known you all his life, and everyone here respects you. He'll listen to you."

Santiague smiled broadly as I spoke. His smile is big and open. He said he would intervene, and as far as I know Gelik hasn't struck the women since. Maybe Santiague used his status as a *gangan*. Maybe he just spoke to Gelik as older man to younger one. All I know is that it seemed to work. The last time Gelik spoke to me, he told me that he wasn't "doing that anymore."

Santiague and Mémé

≈ 14 ≈

Judge and Jury

Martinière received a call on a Thursday night. Ifania had been beaten up by her husband, Grenn. She was hurt, though not badly enough to need emergency care, and she and Grenn had been separated for the night. As far as we could determine from the neighbors we could reach by phone, there was no further immediate danger. We would have to act quickly, but it could wait until the next day.

Friday morning, four of us got on our motorcycles. We hurried from our base in Saut d'Eau across downtown Mirebalais onto the straight, two-lane highway to Domon. There we turned onto the road up Mòn Dega and zigzagged up the steep and dusty series of hills in a line of noise, spewing gravel and exhaust fumes. The delegation included Martinière, Orweeth, Lissage, and me.

When we arrived, we found Ifania and Grenn, with over a dozen of their neighbors, in front of the *ajoupa* where the couple lives with their two little boys. An *ajoupa* is a tent made of straw, the smallest, least substantial sort of housing that we see in the countryside. Ifania is in her mid-twenties, short, dark and slender. She's a quiet woman, dominated in her own *lakou* by Grenn's loud mother Anita, who is also a CLM member.

A *"grenn"* is a seed, usually something small and hard: a coffee bean or a kernel of corn or a cherry pit or even a testicle. Grenn is short and thin. If he had been small from infancy, that might explain why his mother had decided to call him Grenn.

The Mòn Dega road is a long series of climbs, but the ridge where Nan Mango sits is wide and flat. Market days are Wednesday and Saturday, so on Friday it was empty except for the couple of large trees that dot it.

We stepped through a cactus barrier into Ifania's *lakou* and started shaking hands. This took some time, because each of us had to shake hands and exchange greetings with every adult there. A few of the neighborhood's older men suggested that we stand around under the roof of the new house that we were helping the couple to build. Its support posts were up, and its tin roofing was in place. Only the walls remained to be filled in. There was space underneath it for a few of us. Most of the audience would just have to deal with the morning sun.

Lissage took charge of the gathering very simply. As the round of greetings was winding down, he just started to talk, explaining our decision to rush up Mòn Dega. No one else seemed to know quite what they wanted to say, so they just gave way to his direction. The meeting became our meeting from the start. In Creole, "*li saj*" means "he's wise," or "he's polite," but everyone just calls Lissage "S."

S is a farmer and community health worker from Boucan Carré, one of the three areas where we launched the program's pilot. When we first started working near his home, we learned quickly to count on him for support. He was our guide through the entire selection process. He made it possible for us to stay in touch with members on the days when their case managers would not see them. He was diligent in keeping an extra eye on the women who lived near him, helping to ensure that they stuck to the rules that their success would depend on even when their case manager wasn't around. His enthusiasm made it easy for women who had known him for years to trust our team. It was an important part of the pilot's early success.

When we had a sudden need to replace a case manager, S stepped in. Unlike most of the people we hire, he didn't need the job. He could have earned more with his fields and livestock if he really took the time to work them. But he had always wanted to devote himself to helping the poor families living around him. Joining our team gave him a powerful way to do so. He's a dark man with big eyes and a big smile. His short arms and legs are strangely angular, all elbows and knees when he moves. But he waddles so quickly that few can keep up with him.

S turned the discussion with Ifania and Grenn into a hearing. There would be little chance of encountering Haitian law enforcement in an area like Nan Mango. The police stay in the towns, except for the few who are scattered in outposts along the national highways. Local elected officials can appoint deputies to help manage simple disputes in rural areas, but they too can live a long way from the people who elect them. They often move into larger towns, where they find more business opportunities and better education for their kids.

As S began to speak, the whispering going on around us came to a gradual stop. He had our attention. He wasn't loud, but there was an angry edge to his voice. He started by explaining that we do not permit members of our program to behave badly toward their family members or neighbors, but neither will we accept their suffering any sort of abuse. They are our sisters, our mothers, and our daughters as well. We stand by them. He said that we had come because we heard that Ifania had been beaten up. We could see her swollen face and arm. We wanted to get to the bottom of things. Both she and Grenn would have the chance to tell their sides of the story.

Ifania's eyes were glued to the ground in front of her. But Grenn was nervous. He kept talking to the other young men next to him. S had to stop now and again to tell him to quiet down.

When S finished, he asked Ifania to tell us what happened. She stood quietly, and Grenn started to answer, but S cut him off. "We'll listen to you," S explained, "but we want to hear Ifania's story first."

It took some encouragement and some patience, but she finally started to talk. She started in a whisper, but grew stronger as her anger overcame her hesitation. She stood next to S, and looked now again and again toward Martinière, the one of us she knew well. He was standing silently in the background with his big arms crossed, glaring. He is an emotional man, and was too angry with Grenn to speak.

Ifania explained that the problem started when she noticed that 500 gourds were missing. She had hidden the money in a corner of the *ajoupa*, folded under some laundry. The discovery came just after Grenn had asked her for the same amount to help him get to Port au Prince, where he had been offered a week of construction work. When she told him that she couldn't give him the money, he got mad. Shortly after that, the money disappeared.

Grenn interrupted her more than once, but S would remind him that it was his wife's turn to talk, and then Ifania would push on. When she noticed her loss, she looked through the laundry pile and discovered that not just 500, but 1,500 gourds were gone. She had been saving the money by putting aside a portion of her weekly stipend. The pile of laundry was the closest thing to a lockbox that she owned. She had been counting on the fact that she did all the laundry for herself, Grenn and the kids. She didn't think that anyone would rummage through her dirty clothes.

When she realized that her money was missing, she confronted Grenn, but he denied having taken anything. She later went across the road to his mistress's house, and asked her about the money. The mistress, rather than telling Ifania that she didn't know what she was talking about, said that when a man gives her money, it's hers to keep.

That's all that Ifania needed to hear. She started screaming, raising a ruckus. Grenn then tried to drive her out of the other woman's yard. In the struggle, Grenn hit her in the face. As he was dragging her back to their house, he wrenched her arm. When they got back, he continued to hit her, pushing her hard enough into the corner of their *ajoupa* that it collapsed.

Grenn was frightened by what he had done, and he ran off to spend the night with his stepbrother. Ifania found a kind, older neighbor who helped her stand the *ajoupa* back up so that she and her little boys would have a place to sleep.

A couple of times as Ifania was telling her story, Grenn got angry and started to leave, but S would call him back. Grenn would start shouting his defenses and explanations while Ifania was talking.

At one point, S got fed up. "Orweeth, call the justice of the peace down in Boucan Carré. Ask him whether we should bring Grenn to jail in Domon or Chanbo."

It was a great bluff. Orweeth played along, and the two of them made a credible show of it. Orweeth walked partway down the road to get a cell phone signal as soon as S spoke. Before long, we could see him in the distance, pretending to dial a number on his phone.

The older men following the proceedings surrounded Grenn, telling him to settle down. He tried to argue, but they all had an eye on Orweeth. S just stood with his arms crossed, staring Grenn down. When Grenn was calm, the men asked S to give Grenn another chance, and S called Orweeth back. By then, Orweeth was holding his cell phone to his ear, talking, or pretending to talk, with someone. But he shrugged his shoulders, and headed back to rejoin us in the *lakou*.

Now it was Grenn's turn to tell the story, and his version was nothing like Ifania's. He said that she was making a lot of noise over nothing. "*M pat goumen avè l,*" he insisted. "I didn't fight with her." On the contrary, she had fallen while trying to attack the other woman. Either she had lost the money or still had it because he didn't know anything about it.

"*Se mwen menm ki gason nan kay la. Mwen bay kòb, m pa pran l nan men l.*"

"I'm the man," he protested. "I give her money. I don't take it away."

He explained that he was the one who bought the lumber – both support posts and roofing planks – for their new house, and he was the one who carried it all to their *lakou*. He also added a pig and a goat to the livestock we gave her, and was taking care of both her animals and his.

I'm making the proceedings sound clearer and more orderly than they were. There were multiple interruptions. Three or four people would talk at once.

S listened to everything, occasionally asking a probing question or two. Orweeth would say something now and again as well. He's a chatty man, and would repeat things that others had said and add his commentary while others were talking. Martinère kept to the background, glaring at Grenn.

Grenn was excited, repeating the same explanations over and over. "I bought a pig. I bought a goat. And I take care of all the animals. I carried every support post and every plank of lumber here on my head. I'm the man. I give. I don't take." Ifania tried to interrupt him a couple of times. But she was standing right next to me, and I would hold her hand as I reminded her to give Grenn his turn to speak just as she had received hers.

S was ready to announce his decision even before Grenn and Ifania's neighbors were done talking. It was as though he had heard enough to make up his mind. But he waited until he could tell that Grenn had been able to say all he wanted to say. Then it was S's turn. Grenn would have to replace the 1,500 gourds Ifania had lost.

He later told me that he was convinced Grenn had taken the money, but that isn't what he said to the assembled group because he couldn't prove it. S was careful to repeat several times that he was not convicting Grenn of theft. Calling someone a *"volè,"* or "thief," is one of the worst things you can say in Haiti.

But even without calling him a thief, S argued that Grenn was responsible for the loss. After all, he explained, by taking a mistress right across the path from his wife's house, Grenn was asking for trouble, especially since he wasn't able to provide for Ifania and her children.

"I'm not here to tell any man that he can't have two or three women. But you have to be able to take care of them all. *Chyen grangou pa jwe.*" "A hungry dog doesn't play." It was, he said, only natural that Ifania, living in poverty with their two boys, would be sensitive to signs that Grenn was spending their money outside their home. If Ifania hadn't been provoked, S reasoned, she wouldn't have gotten angry enough to lose track of her money.

S ruled that in addition to replacing the money, Grenn would have to take Ifania to the local Partners in Health hospital near Chanbo for a checkup, just to confirm that the beating had done her no serious harm. The care would be free of charge, but the hike would be long. It would throw them together for a day, and give Grenn a chance to demonstrate that he still feels responsible for Ifania's wellbeing.

Grenn accepted the ruling, and said he would sell his pig to give Ifania the money that very day.

Here S did something especially smart: He refused to let Grenn make the sale, realizing that Grenn had already committed the pig to Ifania and her kids. Selling it to give her cash would not help her since, at least informally, it was already hers. There's a Haitian proverb: *"Lave men, siye atè."* "Wash your hands and wipe them off in the dirt." S convinced Ifania to let Grenn owe her the money instead, committing himself to paying her out of his earnings when he returned from Port au Prince.

What was most striking in it all was the authority that S was able to wield. He has no official status in Nan Mango, or anywhere else for that matter, but he was accepted as judge and jury. I thought of the way Pascal had confiscated Louisimène's money. He had shown a sense of authority that I could hardly have imagined. But there,

Pascal was dealing with a woman whom he'd been working with for months, one who might be accustomed to looking to him as her guide.

The improvised trial in Nan Mango was different. No one there knew S well. One can't help but feel that if he had hiked up the hill on his own, things would have been different. But instead he came to a secluded, rural neighborhood at the head of a team of four men on loud motorcycles.

Our team's last words, after the matter was settled, were my own. I said that, as a foreigner, it was not my place to make decisions for Haitians, but that I was responsible for my whole team and that my team's job was to support families who need us. I added that if I needed to come up the mountain with four or five guys to do that, I would. If I needed ten or 20 or 30, I'd do that too.

It was a threat, and I spoke it looking Grenn right in the eyes. We stood close, face to face, as though our conversation was only between us two. I said that, as far as I understood things, he and Ifania had come to an agreement, but that nothing like this better happen again. Grenn promised me that it never would. Our team then got up to leave, and we were careful to shake hands with Grenn and wish him well. We also made sure that Ifania understood that we would come whenever she needed us.

We may be naïve, but we decided to believe that he and Ifania would be able to patch things up. They had been together for seven years, and Martinière said that Grenn was generally one of the most cooperative of the husbands he works with. Martinière had never seen signs of abuse before, nor were any prior incidents mentioned at our hearing. Most importantly, during our long conversation, Ifania showed no inclination either to leave Grenn or to kick him out of her house. We would have supported her in either decision. But it is likely that Ifania will have a better chance to move her family forward economically with a partner's help, and all of Martinière's previous experience of Grenn showed him to be a willing and capable contributor. So if, through a combination of coaxing and intimidation, we were able to get Grenn back on her side, it will likely be for the best.

CLM homes: before the program and after it

⇒ 15 ⇐

Jean Manie's New Home

Jean Manie sparkles when she speaks, even when her energy belies her words. The first time we met, I couldn't get much more out of her than, "*M pa gen anyen pyès, non.*" Or, "I have nothing at all." But she smiled cheerfully as she repeated the line in her high-pitched, singsong-y voice.

At the time, she didn't have a home of her own, not even a beat-up *ajoupa*. Though a woman in her mid-twenties, and mother of an eight-year old boy, she was her cousin's dependent. She had grown up as an orphan, living with her aunt, and when the aunt's daughter married a man from Chimowo named Moussa, Jean Manie had moved with Madan Moussa into her new home.

Jean Manie was a *restavèk*.

Restavèk are children in Haiti who live in domestic servitude. Some are orphans, like Jean Manie, taken in by family members, neighbors or others when their parents die. Many are like Alta, the young mother of two from Viyèt whom I met early in the selection process. They have living parents who give them up because they cannot afford to feed them.

Our program is full of women who grew up as *restavèk*. Born into families that have long been extremely poor, their parents make the desperate choice to give up a child. By the time we come upon most of them, women like Alta and Rose Marthe, they are mothers with their own households.

Jean Manie was different.

She was still living as a *restavèk* when we met her. She owned nothing: no land, no livestock. She owned neither a radio nor a flashlight. She didn't even own the straw mat she would roll out on the floor every night to sleep on.

She was not working full time. She was working all the time. Starting the fire, hauling the water, and emptying and washing the chamber pots early in the morning. After that, she'd prepare the first meal of the day. Then she'd collect the laundry or head out into Moussa's fields. She was paid nothing except the food she ate. She would rise before dawn, and that would be the beginning of a long day filled with nothing but work.

But we couldn't just sign her up for our program. Jean Manie's boy Patrick wasn't living with her. We only work with families. The women we select must be responsible for at least one child. Moussa had put Patrick out of his house when he was a toddler, saying that he would feed Jean Manie, but not her son. So Jean Manie had sent Patrick away to her aunt's house, where she would visit him now and again, whenever she really missed him. But she and her first case manager, Sandra, spoke with Moussa, and he agreed to let Jean Manie bring Patrick back so that we could begin to work with his mother.

Moussa was excited when we invited Jean Manie to join us. He's a farmer. He and his family depend on the land and the livestock he owns. His fields of corn, millet and beans produce more than enough to feed his household. His wife brings the excess to market for sale. And his goats, pigs, cows, and poultry provide steady income as well. He thought that the program would add to his wealth. When he learned that we would be giving Jean Manie goats and a pig, he said they we could just put them together with his. He and his boys would take care of them for her. When he heard that we'd help Jean Manie build a house, he said we could construct it on his land, right in the *lakou* next to his own. None of this seemed to aim at anything that would inconvenience him.

Things did not begin to unravel until he realized that our program was a chance for Jean Manie to break free. By that time, she had a new case manager. Alancia is a tall, powerfully built woman with large, round eyes. A single mother in her late twenties, she had joined Fonkoze as a credit agent, one of the few who are women. Weekdays, she had to leave her boy Joshua in Port au Prince in her family's hands so that she could work in the countryside. She would be with him only on weekends. But she turned out to be very good at her job. She transferred from the credit staff to our team when another member of the staff decided that the physical demands of the job were too much to deal with. There was too much hiking. The roads that we ride our motorcycles on were too difficult. Alancia is strong and tough, and she had little trouble with the rocks and mud she had to face every day.

Alancia made sure that Moussa understood that everything we were giving Jean Manie was for her, not for him and his wife. We had taken Jean Manie into the program hoping to help her develop into an independent adult. As long as she remained a dependent in his home, she did not need us.

Alancia couldn't frame things quite that clearly. She had to spin the truth to make it easier to swallow. She would explain how important it was for Jean Manie to learn to take responsibility, and Moussa and his wife would tell her that they understood. But Alancia's real message must have been all too clear. The couple could see that they stood to lose their unpaid help.

Moussa agreed to cooperate with Alancia, and to let her work with Jean Manie. He presented himself *in loco parentis*, as the adult who had been raising his wife's cousin ever since she was a young girl. But he persistently interfered with the progress Jean Manie was struggling to make. He would send her out into his fields all day, forcing her to leave her livestock in Patrick's hands. Patrick didn't know how to take care of the animals, and he was too small to do so without adult direction and help. The goats were soon in bad shape. Jean Manie's pig had piglets, but they died of neglect, and the sow died shortly after its young.

That's when Claude entered the picture.

We establish committees of local leaders in the communities where we work. Committee members volunteer all sorts of support. They help members get in touch with case managers on days when the case manager is not scheduled to visit, they keep an eye on members' livestock, and they help resolve conflicts among members or between members and their neighbors. The representative for Chimowo was Claude.

We try to get a range of leaders on these committees. Local landowners, small businesspeople, health workers, and elected officials. People who might be able to offer different kinds of help to our members. Claude is a farmer. Not wealthy, but with enough land to support his wife and kids. He also teaches in a small primary school right on the main road that winds from Chanbo to the Feyobyen market. He was able to help some of our families get their children into the school and arrange for Alancia to use the school for training sessions.

He's a small, prematurely balding man with a quick smile and a soft, high-pitched voice that leaves you wondering how he manages a schoolroom full of kids. Claude and Alancia made a funny-looking team. She would tower over him as they chatted about their plans.

They watched helplessly as Jean Manie's pig died and her goats' condition deteriorated. And their problems increased as Jean Manie and Alancia started thinking about her house. Alancia didn't want Jean Manie to accept Moussa's offer to build the house on his land. For her to live in her own separate building, while remaining a part of Moussa's household, would have been no great improvement.

As Alancia started helping Jean Manie look for someplace else to build, Moussa did what he could to hold on to her. Jean Manie would go to church on Sundays with Moussa and the rest of his family, and Alancia got an initial agreement from the church's pastor to sign over a very small corner of church land to Jean Manie. But when Moussa heard about the arrangement, he went to the pastor and threatened to leave the congregation if the pastor followed through. Rather than lose a relatively wealthy congregant, the pastor apologetically went back on his word.

One day, things took a turn for the worse when Madan Moussa sent Jean Manie to Mirebalais, where she and Moussa keep a second home for their children who are in high school. Jean Manie was to do the children's laundry. Normally, they would have paid her transportation and given her something to eat. But at the end of the day, they were angry. The young people accused Jean Manie of ruining a new shirt, and they refused to give her the money she'd need to pay her transportation back to Chimowo. They didn't even feed her. She had to hike several hours home on an empty stomach, after a long day scrubbing their dirty clothes.

Even then, however, Jean Manie couldn't really get herself to decide to leave the family. She and Patrick had nowhere else to go. She was stuck with Moussa and his wife. Theirs was the only home she knew.

But matters came to a head over Jean Manie's goats. Alancia could see the goats were dying. She convinced Jean Manie to turn them over temporarily to Claude. He was willing to look after them, to nurse them back to health, at least until Alancia and Jean Manie could find a more permanent solution.

Moussa was furious. He hadn't been consulted. What's more, he still thought the goats should be in the hands of his younger boys. They could look after them, and then be paid for their work. Typically, someone who keeps a female goat for its owner will receive one of the kids. Moussa wasn't at home when he learned of the decision that Alancia and Jean Manie had made, but he sent Jean Manie a threat. "*M ap gonfle kò w ak baton an.*" That's like saying, "I'll beat you black and blue."

But Jean Manie told Alancia about the threat right away, so Alancia was able to answer Moussa quickly with a threat of her own. She sent him a message: "*Si w mete men w sou Jean Manie, w ap konnen sa m peze.*"

That's a little hard to translate. Literally, it means, "If you lay a hand on Jean Manie, you'll know what I weigh, or how much I can lift." Alancia was saying, "Touch her, and you'll see what I can do. "

The threat was vague, but it worked. Rather than call the bluff of a woman who dwarfs him and would have the entire Fonkoze team behind her, he decided to be done with the whole thing. He kicked Jean Manie and Patrick out of his home once and for all. When Jean Manie got back that afternoon, she found her few possessions – mostly just clothes – scattered in front of the house. She tied them up in a sheet, and went off with the bundle in one hand and Patrick holding the other to find someone who would let them use a cell phone to call Alancia and ask her what to do.

In a sense, we were delighted. Even though Jean Manie would never prosper under Moussa's roof, it had been hard for her to make the decision to leave. Now Moussa had made it for her. But that didn't make her situation easy. Jean Manie had no home of her own.

So Alancia arranged for Jean Manie and Patrick to move in temporarily with another woman in the program who had just finished constructing her new home. Tona was sharing her one room with her two kids, but she was willing to lend a corner of her house to Jean Manie and Patrick. Idana finished building her two-room house soon after that, and Jean Manie and Patrick then moved in with her instead, even though Idana had four children and a husband with her.

But none of that offered anything like a permanent solution, and this is where Claude's commitment really began to show. He owns several pieces of land, and agreed to sign over to her a small *plasman*, a space just big enough to build a house on. Jean Manie's would barely be enough for a little house, a kitchen, and a latrine. But it would be hers.

Our program, however, does not build homes. We provide roofing material and some money to pay builders, but the families we work with have to supply the lumber and the material – palm wood planks or rocks and dirt – that are used to build up the walls.

This would be challenging for Jean Manie because she had no resources of her own to work with. Her livestock was in bad shape. Her pig had died, and the goats were too sick to start producing young. She had received her regular weekly stipend during the first six months of the program, but after making a small deposit into the bank account that her case manager opened for her, she would give the rest to Moussa's wife to "hold onto." Haitians frequently save money by leaving it in wealthier neighbors' hands. But Jean Manie would never see the money again. It would go to repaying debts that Madan Moussa would invent. When the pig died, Madan Moussa had helped Jean Manie sell the meat, but Jean Manie hadn't seen that money by the time she needed to start building. She hadn't been able to organize any new wealth she could use to buy lumber or other materials, and she had no other land where she could harvest the little bit of lumber she would need.

So Claude cut the lumber for Jean Manie on his own land, and helped her carry it to the small plot he had given her. The plot itself had all the dirt and rocks she would need for walls. Jean Manie had to prepare food for the workman who did the building, which would be a big expense by her standards, but also a contribution she was capable of. She also hauled the water they would need to build up the mud walls. She and Patrick moved into the house as soon as the first of its two small rooms was ready. She didn't even wait to install a door.

Jean Manie and Patrick were finally in their own home, and they were very happy about it. Jean Manie expressed her feelings simply: "When you're in your own home, if you're not feeling well in the morning, you just stay in bed. When you live in someone else's home, you have to get up every morning, no matter how sick you are." Patrick put things more starkly than that, "Even if they just sent me on an errand to Moussa's house, I'd rather die than go." Strong words from an eight-year-old.

Marie

≥ 16 ≤

More about Marie Paul

One day, Martinière came back late to our base in Saut d'Eau from Mannwa in a little bit of a panic. He hadn't been able to find Marie Paul. When he went by her house, already late in the afternoon, he saw three of her younger kids, obviously hungry. The baby was crawling around the unswept yard, putting whatever it came across into its mouth. The older kids were out and about, probably scavenging, trying to figure out what they might find to eat either among their neighbors or in the gleanings of nearby fields.

So he asked around, and heard a disturbing rumor. Marie Paul had sold her goats and cashed out her small business. She was back to zero.

The livestock and merchandise we give to our members is theirs to keep, but they are not supposed to dispose of it without our permission. They even sign an agreement to that effect. In February, I had been worried that Marie was handling her cash stipend so carefully that her children were still going hungry. Now we were hearing that she had sold out and spent everything. It didn't make sense.

Martinière had then spoken to Edrès, who had heard the same rumor. Edrès added that he hadn't been able to talk with Marie yet, but had sent her a message. He told her teenage boy Ezechiel that he needed to see her.

Edrès has no legal authority in Mannwa. He's not an elected official, nor has he ever been appointed to any official post. But he's a relatively wealthy neighbor who shows that he cares about the people around him, so people like Marie look to him. He's earned a measure of authority by proving his goodwill. She wouldn't be likely to duck him for very long, but he was worried because she hadn't come to see him right away.

Wednesday was always Martinière's most difficult day. The hike from our residence in Zaboka was long, so he had to start early. It wasn't much of a base, just a 12-by-12-foot room with thin mattresses on the hard, uneven dirt floor. Whenever I was with them, there would be five of us trying to sleep on those mattresses. And two of us snored.

But Martinière would get up especially early on Wednesdays, because he had more than an hour's walk even to start the day. He'd hike up out of Zaboka to the top of Gwo Monte and then down to and across the river that separates eastern Tit Montay from the rest of Boucan Carré. Finally, he'd head back up toward the Mannwa ridge. Curling around the northwest side of the hill as he climbed, he'd get to Wòch Djèp, where he'd see Rose Marthe, his first visit in Mannwa. After spending some time with her, he'd have to walk up and down the series of secondary ridges that run north and south behind Mannwa. Threading his way from ridge to ridge, he would visit the next three women. It would be midday by the time he could get to the top of Mannwa to see four more families. Then he'd have another four families to see in two separate neighborhoods on the south side, having to hike halfway down the hill and back up again, twice, to find them. He would have left Zaboka by six in the morning, getting a snack on his way out the door, and wouldn't get to the residence in Saut d'Eau and a real meal until five or six at night. The day was hard in the best of times, but during rainy season getting drenched would be the least of his problems. Riding his motorcycle through several inches of mud down the road out of Viyèt would be work hard enough to exhaust most people all by itself. And he would be doing it at the end of a long, foodless day.

But it wouldn't exhaust Martinière. Nothing exhausts Martinière.

And that's not even what's striking about him.

What's most striking about him is, first, how much he cares. He gets passionate about all the details of his work with families. He's excitable: jolly when things are going well, sullen and quick to anger if things are going wrong.

But the second striking thing about him, quieter but equally important, is his intense curiosity. He shows every day that he approaches his work as a learner, anxious for any little lesson he might pick up as he listens or works.

The walk to Marie's house, on the northeastern side of the Mannwa ridge, was out of the way. She didn't live near any of the other families we were working with. Martinière had hiked the extra half hour he needed to get to Marie's house and back to no purpose. We needed to speak with her, and we didn't think it could wait a week for Martinière`s next visit. But he had a full schedule, so I went to Mannwa a few days later, hoping to find her. I too failed.

Since we had a three-day workshop planned for all members, we decided just to focus on getting her to the training. I left a message with Edrès, asking him to tell her that we were concerned and that we really needed to talk to her. We wanted her to know that we very much wanted to see her at the training. He said that he'd be certain to send her word.

Fortunately, she decided to come. And she told us the following story:

She and her first husband had struggled to send Ezechiel to school. She somehow continued to send the boy even after her husband died, but when it was time for Ezechiel to take the official primary school graduation exam, she was out of money. She owed the school 1,750 gourds, less than $45, and the principal was holding her boy's exam ticket in lieu of payment. Ezechiel, by then in his teens, wouldn't be able to take the exam unless she could pay the bill.

She couldn't bear the thought that he might have to stop without even taking the exam. She, her late husband, and the boy himself had gone through too much. So she borrowed the money, hoping to repay the loan with a bean harvest. Unfortunately, rats infested her field.

As time passed, and she saw that she had no hope of repaying her debt, she disappeared. The shame, the sense of hopelessness, was too much. She moved to La Chappelle, farther down the Artibonite River to the west, hoping she'd have a better chance of finding the money she'd need.

When her lender from Mannwa found her there, she turned to a loan shark in La Chappelle. By then, she was together with her second husband. He had just planted a crop of pigeon peas, and he told her she could sell the harvest to pay back the loan. So she took the loan and repaid her original debt even though she had to agree to 100% interest every six months. Having cleared her first debt, she was able to return to her home in Mannwa.

But rats again ate her harvest.

And then the man abandoned her, and she was left once more without a way to repay what she owed. Interest kept accumulating. By the time we began working with her just a couple of years later, her original debt of 1,750 gourds had grown to more than 8,000.

The loan shark was probably starting to lose hope. Marie would not be able to pay money she didn't have. But then he discovered that she was part of some program that had given her livestock, and even some cash. She had the three goats we had given her along with a fourth she had purchased with savings from her weekly food stipend. They were all pregnant. He went to Mannwa together with a local deputy to get his money back. He took her goats, she said, and sold them. The debt was thus erased, but the loss was a big setback, even though Marie Paul added that her small business was still intact.

The next time Martinière had a free day, he decided to hike up to Mannwa to see her, and I decided to go along. Though she knew we were coming, we once again failed to find her at home. We found Ezechiel instead, and he told us that she was down in Laplenn Twou

Lanfè, or Hellhole Plain, in the depths of the broad, grassy valley behind Mannwa.

As we descended the long, winding path, Martinière started yelling to Marie long before my myopic eyes could see her at all. Martinière has a booming voice, so he was able to get her attention. She started up the path to meet us as we continued down the hill.

We came upon her as we made the last of a series of blind, hairpin turns down the gravelly foot path. She was coal black from her elbows to her fingertips. Her face was covered with coal dust as well, except where descending drops of perspiration had traced lighter colored lines down her cheeks. She didn't want to accept the respectful kiss on the forehead that we would normally greet her with. She was, she said, too dirty. But we kissed her anyway, and then started to talk.

Martinière wanted first to hear about her business. She had used her money to buy a tree that she was converting to charcoal, and had hired someone to cut the tree to pieces. He made a neat pile of the wood, and then buried it to burn. Marie was uncovering the charcoal and putting it into sacks. She said she had nine sacks ready for sale, five in a warehouse in the market in Difayi, on the nearest major road below Mannwa, and four more she'd be moving to market in the next days. It would be worth something like 1,800 gourds, already a nice profit over the 1,500 gourds she started with. She wasn't finished, so when we were done talking, she turned back down to her charcoal, and Martinière and I turned back up the hill.

But this is where things get complicated.

We had asked Edrès to find out what he could, and we stopped to chat with him when we got back up to Mannwa. He told us a different story about her goats. He said that she had borrowed money to pay for a funeral. One of her children had died a few years previously, struck by lightning. The rest of the story corresponded more or less with what she had said, except that he added that he had heard that the loan shark had threatened her life.

We also spoke to Ezechiel, who told us that the loan shark had not seized the goats, but had pressured Marie to pay him. Ezechiel said that she had taken the goats to the market in Regalis, and sold them there. He also told us that she had gone down the mountain to Difayi a few days previously with one sack of charcoal, not five.

We couldn't be sure that Marie was telling us the truth. But we needed to know just what her situation was. Otherwise, we would not be able to help her.

So Martinière told her to have the proceeds from her charcoal sales ready to show him on his next visit. But when we went by as scheduled on the following Wednesday, once again she wasn't there.

She appeared to be ducking us.

We weren't sure what to do next. We decided to wait for the Mannwa Village Assistance Committee's next meeting, scheduled for the last Wednesday of the month. All the women from the neighborhood who were part of the program would be there. Edrès was president of the committee, and we wanted both him and the other members to be part of the conversation. We also asked him to have the deputy there. We wanted to hear his version of the story, too. And we would come with Emile, one of our senior case managers, who had been trained as a lawyer.

Lots of Haitians speak quickly. Creole is a language that lends itself to contraction. Syllables take the place of words, and letters take the place of syllables. "I don't know what he said" might start as *"Mwen pa konnen, ki sa li te di."* But then it turns into *"M pa konnen, sa l te di"* or *"M pa konn, sa l di."* And Emile speaks especially quickly. He communicates very effectively with fellow Haitians of all kinds, but I knew him for years before I was able to understand him consistently and well.

Emile organized the meeting as a hearing, much as S had done when we were trying to help Ifania and Grenn. He had everyone sit in a circle in the shade in front of Edrès's small home. He grilled Marie in front of them, cornering her with her conflicting stories.

He and Edrès quickly got her to admit that her initial claim that the loan shark had taken and sold her goats was false. She had sold them herself.

When we found out that Marie had been lying, we could have kicked her out of the program. She had already been making herself very difficult to work with. Again and again, Martinière would go by her home midday on Wednesday and discover that she wasn't there. He was frustrated.

I am a former college dean of students, and I occasionally had to deal with young people unwilling or unable to respect our school's rules, so I sometimes have the inclination to expel. At a college, kicking students out can be the right thing to do, both for them and for the school.

But this just doesn't work for CLM. Marie was in our program because her family desperately needed it. Her children were hungry. They weren't eating even once a day. Ezechiel was continuing to put himself through school by taking off weeks at a time to work for neighbors in their fields. But because he couldn't be in school all the time, he hadn't passed the previous year, and had to repeat the class. None of his younger siblings were going to school at all. This was all the harsher because the church right in front of their home had an inexpensive little school within it. Inexpensive, but not free. It was thus beyond Marie's means. But her children would see their friends and neighbors come to school in their little uniforms every day.

Emile asked the women at the meeting what they thought we should do. There was some discussion, but Rose Marthe and Sorène felt very strongly and their opinions carried the day. Sorène said we couldn't kick Marie out. She had sold her goats because a man had come threatening her with a machete. It hadn't been her fault. Rose Marthe blamed Marie because she hadn't tried to go to anyone for help, but she couldn't blame her for selling her goats at the point of a knife.

At the same time, we couldn't just replace the assets she had lost. Apart for the fact that we are limited by our budgets, we cannot afford to have members think that they can do what they want with their assets because we'll always just buy new ones for them. Marie had lost all of her assets, so we needed to find an approach that would help her start over again. She and Martinière would have their work cut out for them.

Josamène

⇒ 17 ⇐

Josamène Loréliant

The first time I went looking for Josamène, I had a hard time finding her. Martinière and I had been hiking around the neighborhoods just below Mannwa for most of a day. He was a new case manager, and I was showing him around. He's a big man. Not enormous, but big. And his outsized personality only makes him seem even larger than he is. He has strength, a big heart, and lots of force of character. His willingness to use all three for the families he serves has become something of a watchword among us. Our boss, Gauthier, calls him "*Vayan.*" That means "brave" or "tough." It can also mean "bully." At the time, however, I had just met him and didn't know what to expect.

Mannwa is strictly agricultural, very rural, and has no roads. Narrow footpaths lead up, down and around its steep slopes. Like much of Haiti, it has lost its tree cover. Though the island was once a thick forest, there is very little of that left on the Haitian side. Intense farming, the constant demand for lumber for construction and furniture, and the need for cooking fuel have eliminated most of Haiti's trees. During the rainy season in Mannwa, small plots of beans, corn and millet alternate with wild grasses. During the dry season, the grayish brown soil crumbles into hard granules and dust.

Martinière and I were on the southern face of the ridge, about 20 or 30 minutes down from the top. Our long day of hiking was almost over. We had traversed Mannwa's southern base to see a number of members in Boukankola, a series of small valleys to the west, and then hiked most of the way up to the ridge. Getting to the people we'd need to see in the last two neighborhoods would involve hiking halfway back down the hill and then up again. Twice. And we were both dragging.

Josamène's house – such as it was – was hidden between trees, about 50 feet off the narrow path that ran up and down the hill. The nearest neighbors were higher up the hill and farther off the path. We were climbing up from below, and we couldn't see any homes. I was a couple of steps ahead of Martinière as we forced ourselves up the narrow, winding path. The dusty, baseball-sized rocks strewn along it made for treacherous footing. I had a wide vista of Central Boucan Carré behind my back as we climbed, and a mix of tall grasses and occasional trees above me, but I saw none of it. My eyes were on the ground, helping me find the spots where I could safely place my feet.

We were within a few hundred yards from her home, but no one in the neighborhood had ever heard of Josamène, even though she had been living in the same *lakou* for years. They only knew her by her nickname, Ti Rizib.

Nicknames are extremely common in Haiti, especially in rural Haiti. One comes across examples that will surprise anyone unused to them, with meanings that range from the merely perplexing to worse. Sepavre (That's not true), Nawè (We'll See), Kriskapab (Christ is Able), Liserès (He or She is the Leftover), Malgresa (Despite That), and Mizèfanm (A Woman's Suffering) are more or less typical examples. My godson has an aunt who was her parents' seventh daughter. They called her Asefi, which means "Enough Daughters." When her little sister arrived, they nicknamed her Asenèt, or "Enough is Enough."

The names can be confusing, too. A woman we worked with in Bay Tourib is called Sanmoun. I was horrified. "*San*" means "without," and "*moun*" means "person." In general parlance, "*gen moun*" or "to have people" means having family or friends, people you can count on. It is sometimes used the way we say that someone "has connections." When I first heard the name, I thought that "Sanmoun" meant that her very name announced that she was alone in the world. But Gauthier set me straight. It means that she has no person, no body, that there is nothing to her. And Sanmoun is really a tiny wisp of a woman.

But Josamène's nickname, Ti Rizib, is terrible. The Creole word "*rizib*" comes from a French word that means "laughable," but Creole puts an even more cutting spin on it. To call someone Ti Rizib is like calling her a joke. Worse than that, it implies that she's nothing. And Josamène had been living as Ti Rizib all her life.

When we finally located her place, the only person we could find was a girl about 12 or 13 years old, her daughter Ti Wakin. She was short and dark-skinned. Her small, bright eyes shone beneath her broad little forehead. Puberty was just around the corner, but at the moment she still looked like a little girl. That would change over the coming months, right before our eyes.

We didn't need to ask Ti Wakin whether her parents were home. We could see that much for ourselves. The only hut in their yard had a roof made of cracked, sun-bleached *tach*. Its walls were woven of sticks that had once been covered in mud. The roofing was split in numerous places, and the mud from the walls had begun falling off in chunks. The gaps between the bare sticks made it easy to see that the house was empty. We could see most of what was inside it, and some of what was behind it, too. A few pieces of clothing were hanging from rafters or from ropes that had been hung along the walls. We later learned that Josamène had seen us coming and had run off to hide. Her husband, Lwidòn, wasn't there either. He was off working in someone's field.

We spoke with Ti Wakin for a few minutes. She's bright and outgoing, and Martinière had her chatting playfully with him before long. The house is on a flat space that had been cut into the hill years earlier. We were sitting on a straw mat that had been left out to dry in the sun. Martinère looked across at small holes burrowed into the gray, clayey slope, and asked Ti Wakin what they were. When she said that they were tarantula dens, he asked her to reach into one and pull out the spider so that he could see it. *"Mwen menm? Y ap mòde m, wi!"* she answered. "Me? They'll bite!" But she could tell it was in good fun, and his teasing put her at ease.

Our team had already recommended Josamène for our program, but I needed to verify their recommendation before Martinière could invite her to join us. Though I would normally have to interview the prospective member herself before deciding whether she qualified, we were on a very tight schedule. Training was only a few days away, and we needed to get people to it. And we couldn't just wait around because we had three more families to visit and it was getting late. The rains could start at any time. If they started while we were in the field, we would have a very bad time getting our motorcycles down from Viyèt, where we had left them, to the main road in Difayi.

Ti Wakin was old enough to give us clear answers, and didn't seem to be lying. So I approved Josamène provisionally on the basis of what Martinière learned from her daughter, and before we left we told her when and where her mother's training would be. Martinière took pains to make Ti Wakin repeat the message several times.

"Where did we say the training would be?"

"At the school at Kafou Jòj."

"And when will it be?"

"Monday."

"What time did we say?"

"At 8:00."

He made sure that she had the important details just right. She did everything he asked, but showed a lot of eye-rolling, teenage attitude. When we held the workshop a few days later, Josamène showed up, just as we hoped she would.

But she wasn't alone. Ti Wakin came with her. They sat next to one another on one of the rough wooden benches that were arranged into something like a square along the walls of the schoolroom we were using, squeezed in among the other women. Ti Wakin sat straight, while her mother angled her body toward the little girl, as if she wanted to hide behind her. Josamène is a tiny woman, and little Ti Wakin would soon be bigger and taller than she was. Josamène was the one who felt the need for protection.

Women sometimes bring their children to our workshops. They come with infants and small toddlers because they don't know what else they can do with them, or they come with older children, hoping to find a way to get them some of the workshop's free food.

Josamène and Ti Wakin were different. Ti Wakin had not come just for the food, though she was quick to the front of the line whenever food was being served. She has a very robust appetite. She had come to do the talking for her mother. She joined workshop activities with enthusiasm, singing and clapping, while her mother clung silently at her side. Josamène was so intensely shy, so lacking in social skills that she let a girl not yet out of puberty speak in her place. Ti Wakin came with her to the next workshop and the next.

Josamène's struggles are evident as one sits with her. The contours etched into her face seem to reflect years of hardship. Her speech is barely audible. Even after 18 months in our program, she would speak only in short phases that can be hard to understand. She seems never to want to face forward, always turning her head well off to the side. Her large, bright eyes never look directly at you. Nor do they seem to be looking at something else. Instead, they seem only to be looking away.

She and her husband have had 13 children, but only five survived. Sitting in front of their home, Lwidòn looks sadly, but matter-of-factly at the places in their yard where they've buried their kids, "Two here, two there, two over there." He goes through the list as he points out their graves, while Josamène sits silently in the background.

When we first met the family, we had a hard time getting Josamène to talk at all. As we tried to interview her, she kept finding excuses to slip away. Her neighbors told us she was *egare*. That means scatterbrained. Her husband said merely that she *"konn pale anpil."*

Literally, that would mean that she talks a lot. And literally, it was almost exactly false. If anything, Lwidòn is the one who talks a lot. It is no accident that most of what I can quote about them comes from him. Even if you ask her a direct question, he is likely to be the one who responds. He did, and still does, almost all of the talking for both of them. He's a very chatty man. Whether angry or pleased, he has a lot to say.

But *""pale anpil"* means, more loosely, that someone is a little crazy, and Lwidòn explained that Josamène hadn't been the same since the death of her last child, who was killed when their house burned down. It was the second time that they had lost a straw shack to fire, and we have heard rumors that both fires were set. Neighbors had accused the couple of preventing the rain from falling. In an area populated by farmers, mostly poor ones, it's a very serious accusation.

Josamène and Lwidòn were vulnerable to the accusation for two reasons. First, their house was already in such terrible shape that any rain would have soaked them and their children. In other words, if one considers only the state of their home, one might think they would have good reason to block rain. Second, they were perceived as being dirty, and it is believed that those who can stop rain from falling don't bathe. A young friend of mine from the region put things simply. In dry periods, "just because some poor guy looks dirty, they say that he's the one who won't let the rain fall."

On the surface, however, the accusation seems unbelievable, even assuming that someone could have the magical power to control rain. Josamène, Lwidòn, and their children were almost entirely dependent on farming, living off their own meager harvest and the work they could find in neighbors' fields. Any drought would hurt them badly.

But their neighbors didn't see things that way, and crowds ganged up on the two on several occasions. Josamène told me once how a mob had forced her to parade all through Deniza and

Mannwa while they hit her occasionally with a stick. Lwidòn was beaten as well. Maybe their terrible poverty left them looking like suitable scapegoats. I don't know.

Over the years, they had frequently been subject to abuse. Even after they joined our program, they had neighbors who fought to ensure that they would fail. They tried to prevent Josamène from developing the assets that we gave her. She initially received two goats, and neighbors beat one nearly to death, in part to avenge themselves against Lwidòn for having chased their own goats out of his field. His regular inability to farm his own land had left them feeling entitled to use it. Josamène would set a portion of her weekly food stipend apart and would occasionally buy a chicken, but neighbors would steal them. She bought two turkeys, but neighbors killed them with rocks.

Their bad relations with their neighbors also meant that Martinière had to struggle hard to get Josamène and Lwidòn to do everything they would need to do to build their house. Our program is committed to ensuring that every family is living in a house with a tin roof, one that can keep the family dry. Martinière proposed a series of skilled local builders, but Lwidòn would never agree to any of them. He said that he and one candidate after another didn't get along. Eventually, Martinière arranged for builders from Zaboka, more than a two-hour hike from Josamène's yard, to come build the house, but that didn't work either. The day they came, Josamène was at a meeting Martinière had organized, and she left to show the builders where they were to construct her home. When they got there, Lwidòn refused to let them work. He said that the 14 sheets of tin roofing that the program was providing were too few. He would have lots of visitors. Relatives would come to see him. So he would need a much bigger house. He'd wait until he could afford to buy more roofing, and build then.

But Josamène wanted the house built right away. The hut that was standing might have been something like a home, but it was nothing like a shelter. So Martinière argued with Lwidòn. This involved a certain amount of shouting and name-calling on both sides. Martinière is good at yelling, and Lwidòn is no slouch.

Eventually they compromised. Martinière convinced Lwidòn that even if they built a small house for Josamène and the children right now, Lwidòn would always be able to build a larger one later when he and Josamène could afford it. Then they could use the first, smaller one as their kitchen and storeroom. But Josamène and Martinière also agreed to use some of her savings to buy four additional sheets of tin. Lwidòn found a builder he was happy with, and the house went up.

Shortly after it was completed, Josamène had more trouble with her neighbors. The nearest one is a relatively well-to-do farmer named Sadrack. Someone in Sadrack's yard threw rocks at the house, piercing one of the sheets of tin. Martinière needed to act. So he went with Josamène to speak with Edrès, a leader in the community, and asked him to tell Sadrack's family that if there were any more attacks on Josamène, her family or her property, he would have Sadrack arrested. It is not at all certain that he could have made good on his threat, but the threat was enough. There were no further incidents.

⚓ ⚓ ⚓

Before they joined us, Josemène and her household would have food for more or less time after each harvest, depending how good the harvest had been. But for much of the time when their harvest ran out they would simply go hungry, scavenging what they could find from the trees in their yard. The older of her two living sons, Dieupuissant, had fled to Mirebalais even before we met the family. He was hungry, and decided he could do better eking out his own living through whatever activities he might come across in the town's streets. One of Martinière's key challenges as he worked with Josamène was to help her ensure that she would have enough income to enable her to feed her family well year-round.

The first breakthrough came from the way Martinière taught her to use trees that were already growing on their land: coconuts, avocados, key limes, and other valuable fruit. Rather than letting the fruit ripen on the trees so that they could harvest them for sale, they would let their kids eat them early, whenever they were hungry. Their neighbors would help themselves freely as well.

Martinière started by teaching them the value of coconuts. He showed Josamène that she could sell bunches of them by buying them himself to let them sprout to distribute the seedlings to other families nearby. Seeing the income that she and Lwidòn could earn encouraged her to cultivate the coconuts seriously. They began taking bunches to market and selling them, and also planting more trees. Encouraged by that success, she began taking other fruit to market as well.

Helping families lift themselves out of poverty means helping them build income and wealth, but it is a social phenomenon as well. And one aspect of the social change we try to effect involves working on the way members look at themselves. Josamène is a woman who's spent her adult life letting her husband and others speak for her and make decisions for them both. But when Martinière first bought a bunch of coconuts from them, he had only 50 gourds with him. The bunch cost 100, so he could only make a down payment. Josamène wasn't home, so Martinière gave the money to Lwidòn. The next week, Martinière brought money to pay the balance that he owed. When he started to hand the fifty gourds to Lwidòn, Josamène erupted. "I'm the woman. I'm the one who goes to the market. I'm the one who needs cash."

Several months later, more than a year after Josamène joined the program, we were back at Kafou Jòj at the last of our follow-up trainings. I was teaching the group a new game, one designed to help everyone learn their fellow participants' names. You stand in a circle, and the first person introduces herself. The next then introduces both herself and the first person. The third introduces the first two and then herself. You keep going around the circle, each person having to remember more and more names. The last person in the circle goes through every name.

Knowing how bad I am at remembering names, I cheated. I started the circle myself. So it went something like this:

"My name's Steven."

"That's Steven. My name's Mirlène."

"That's Steven. That's Mirlène. My name's Ti Komè."

When Josamène's turn came, I assumed she would let it pass and that Ti Wakin, who was next to her, would speak as usual. Ti Wakin was more than a year older than she had been the day we met, and she was growing fast. She was beginning to look every bit the teenager that she was. She was enjoying the game, laughing as women remembered or failed to remember one another's names.

But when their turn came, it was Josamène who spoke. Her voice was quiet but clear, and her eyes were locked on the ground, near some undefined point in the middle of the circle.

"My name is Josamène Loréliant," she declared. Then she made her way credibly through the names of everyone who had preceded her.

Martinière and I looked at each other. We could hardly believe that Josamène had decided to speak. The game went on. The other women seemed barely to notice what had happened. Most of the women present had known one another for years. Many of them had nicknames, and some were known mainly by their husband's names.

"That's Steven. That's Mirlène. That's Ti Komè. That's Alta. That's Atour. That's Sorène. That's Oranie. That's Jordanie. That's Madan Ti Sourit."

Then it would come to Josamène, and whoever was speaking would say, "That's Ti Rizib."

And Josamène would quietly correctly them. "My name is Josamène Loréliant."

It took several rounds before some of the women started to refer to her as "Josamène." Others continued to call her "Ti Rizib."

"Don't call me that," she finally said.

All through the game, she insisted on the use of her full, real name, Josamène Loreliant, even in the middle of a community of women who had known her only by her nickname for all the decades she had lived among them. When one of the case managers who was present mistakenly referred to her as Ti Rizib later in the meeting, she sniped audibly, "You too?" He apologized immediately. Lwidòn still calls her Ti Rizib, and when I asked Josamène whether that bothers her, she joked, "I ignore him."

When I go by to visit them these days, it takes some time before she will talk with me. Uniquely among hundreds of women I've worked with, when Josamène sees me she disappears into her house. It is no longer because she wants to hide, the way she did the first time I came looking for her. She goes inside to wash her face and put on a clean dress and sandals. She doesn't want me to see her any old way. This is especially striking because of how slovenly I tend to be. But appearance is now important to this woman, who is no longer Ti Rizib.

Ti Wakin and Josamène

PART III:

CHALLENGES TO OVERCOME

"Dèyè mòn gen mòn."
(Beyond mountains there are
[more] mountains.)

Rose Marthe

⇒ 18 ⇐

A Reasonable Chance

Rose Marthe lives near the northern border of the central Haitian county of Boucan Carré. The border runs along a series of ridges. Boucan Carré is rural, and its northern half is mountainous. It has a few neighborhoods of 50 or 100 households that you could perhaps call "villages," but consists mostly of open fields and farmland that either line its many slopes or are squeezed into its narrow valleys. It's lightly sprinkled with *lakou*, the small clusters of two or three or a half-dozen houses usually belonging to a single extended family. *Lakou* are part of the basic structure of rural Haitian life.

During the days, most of the men and many of the women are in the fields, farming much the way their families probably have for generations. They use few tools, maybe just a machete, a pick, a hoe, or a *digo*, a small handheld sickle. They farm even the steepest of slopes, one foot well uphill of the other as they bend down toward the earth, planting or weeding or tilling. Some of the women gather along rocky streambeds, washing clothes and bed linens by hand, their smaller children playing naked nearby, waiting for their one t-shirt or dress or pair of pants to dry. And there is the constant back-and-forth along the many twisting, narrow footpaths, traffic to and from the various rural markets, many of which are accessible only on foot. Merchants load their wares on horses, mules or donkeys, or they carry them on their heads. Men and boys drive goats, pigs and cows to the markets for sale.

I was hiking one day on a footpath that winds along the western end of Do Zoranj, the ridge separating Boucan Carré from the neighboring counties of Maïssade and Hinche to the north. I had climbed the steep, south-facing hill in a neighborhood called Chipen, and was walking eastward toward another called Bwawouj, where I would be able to turn down the northern side of the ridge and head into Regalis, an important but isolated market town in Hinche. From Regalis, I would work my way across to Bay Tourib, in Thomonde, my destination for the day.

The path weaves from one side of Do Zoranj to the other as the peasants who have worn it into the earth have turned through the years to choose the easiest passage. The northern side offers wide views of the Upper Central Plateau. At one moment, I was looking down into the grassy plain of central Maïssade. At another, I was viewing the short but steep hills and narrow valleys that lead downward toward Hinche. On the southern side, the high hills that run throughout Tit Montay leave little more to be seen than bean fields dotted with trees, occasional houses, and clusters of large, exposed rocks. In the distance behind the far eastern end of the ridge, I could occasionally make out Mirebalais, the main town on the lower plateau.

It was a cool day at the beginning of March, toward the end of the dry season. In summer the hillsides would be covered with grass tall enough to hide the footpaths that run along and through them, tall enough in places to hide my 5'10" from anyone who might be walking ahead of or behind me. Now they were bare, except for the beige remnants of dried-up grass. Here and there I passed yellowed bean fields, planted in the hope that dew and occasional drizzle would be enough to sustain them through the winter. The dried leaves and undeveloped pods were proof that not every hope comes true. Nevertheless, farmers were working in the fields, some harvesting their minimal crops and some tilling the soil, as if to demonstrate that hope grows more reliably than beans.

I had started the day in Zaboka, one of the larger villages in northwestern Boucan Carré. I had gone there to see Mersereste, a young woman who was part of a group of CLM members who would soon be graduating in Bay Tourib. She had just moved to Zaboka after deciding to separate herself from her abusive husband, and I wanted to know how she was doing and to see whether she qualified for graduation.

It had been a long hike just to get to Zaboka, taking half a day as I walked over a series of short, steep hills. But I had managed to find Mersereste as soon as I arrived, and was pleased to see that she was doing fairly well. She had moved back into her mother's *lakou*, and had a capable teenage brother who was ready to build her a new house. He had carried her 14 sheets of tin roofing all the way back from Bay Tourib on his head, and had begun to erect a frame. He was also helping her take care of the goats she brought back with her. With graduation just a few weeks away, she wouldn't be ready in time, but she was in good hands.

Since I had managed to see her before sunset, I would have time to spend the whole next day hiking back to Bay Tourib the long way, visiting other families the only way I could reach them, on foot.

Labòd is a two-hour uphill hike from Zaboka, along a narrow footpath that winds between and around rocky bean fields until it sneaks through a narrow pass. I emerged from the pass, and headed downhill into a small valley. The path cut through the valley's center. Edithe saw me as I approached her house, and ran up to greet me, already talking.

She was quick to say "*Bonjou*," but before I could respond with more than a "*Bonjou*" of my own, she was confessing. She didn't even let me ask her about her children. One of her goats and her pig had died since graduation. She told me the story of the goat's slow decline, and of the steps she had taken to try to save it. The pig had died of Teschen Disease, as many all across Central Haiti do. She still had five goats, however, and they were flourishing. Her small cow was healthy and continuing to grow, even though the dry season was making it harder to find forage.

When I finally was able to turn the conversation to her children, she brightened up. She and her six kids were in good health, and she had been able to assemble the money she needed to send the five younger ones to school.

Most importantly, her attitude was hopeful. Though she spoke first about her losses, she wasn't dwelling on them. She was looking ahead. We spoke about the plans she had already thought through for assembling school fees for the following year, even though summer vacation was still months away.

From Edithe's house, I continued across Labòd, fording the small mountain stream that cuts the valley in two. It's shallow during the dry season, barely enough to cover my ankles. But the water runs cold and clear. I crouched down to rinse off my face and my neck and let some run through my very short hair. The tropical mountain sun is fierce, and the water felt good. Once across the stream, I began hiking up the footpath that that leads up the valley's northern side into Chipen.

Chipen is almost all farmland. Jagged red and white boulders peek out from its light grayish-brown soil. Along its few trails, the soil is baked into hard granules in March by months without rain. Here and there, a narrow flat space cuts into the slope and there is a small *lakou* with a couple of houses and the one or two trees that haven't yet been cut down for lumber or charcoal.

Melicia is a tiny old woman who lives halfway up the hillside. Few people know her real name. They call her "*Ti Kout*," which means "Shorty," and the name fits her well. She might be almost 4'10", but is probably shorter than that, even though she stands erect with the strength that allows her to farm her land and carry her harvest to market. She lives with a couple of grandchildren who depend on her for everything they have.

She wasn't home when I arrived in her *lakou*, but a couple of 20-somethings were sitting on rocks in the shade under a tree. They had been working in a neighbor's field. When I asked for Ti Kout, they told me she was off seeing about her pigs, which she keeps down the slope at a son's house. The men had just gotten there, and were happy to take some time to relax. I sat with them for a while, waiting for Ti Kout to return. But I was impatient because I still had a long hike ahead of me. So after a few minutes, I asked them for directions, and I continued up the slope.

Shortly after I started hiking away, I heard a voice yelling from behind me: "*Dirèk! Dirèk!*"

Ti Kout and one of her grandsons were running straight uphill to catch up with me. My title at Fonkoze is "Regional Director," or "*Direktè Rejyonal.*" The people I work with, both the staff and the families we serve, tend to shorten that. I can't generally get them to call me "Steven." But rather than the stiff-sounding "*direktè,*" they call me "*dirèk.*"

It was quite a sight. She is a tiny, grandmotherly woman who looks no younger than her age, and she was sprinting so quickly up the twisting, rocky footpath that her grandson was having trouble keeping up. She was still panting as she explained that she had gotten home just after I left, and was anxious to see me.

We sat on jagged brown rocks as she caught her breath, and I started to ask her about her and the kids. She was happy to report that she had finally managed to send the children to a very small school just across the valley. She quickly described how her livestock had increased. She was doing very well, in fact.

She and her grandson walked me the rest of the way up the hill to make sure I found the right path toward Bwawouj. It meant a lot of extra hiking for them, but she said she was worried that I might get lost, though I'm not sure how I could have. When we got near the top of the hillside, I started to get a cell phone signal. So I called Martinière, who had been her case manager, reaching him in Central Mirebalais, where he was at work with new members. I let Ti Kout talk with him. She grabbed my cell phone like someone who had never used one before, bringing the entire device down to her lips when she wanted to speak, and then returning it to her ear to listen. When she gave me back the phone she was weeping. "I got to hear my Martinière's voice!" she cried.

Orélès and Mirlène

Only at Mirlène's house, the third woman I visited on my rounds that day, did I find reason for serious concern. She and her husband Orélès live right along the ridge above Bwawouj. They have a wide view of the small, elliptical Bwawouj valley on one side of their home, and an even broader one of Regalis, well down the mountain in Hinche, on the other.

I grew worried as I approached the house they built while she was in the program because it appeared abandoned. We offer several different kinds of assistance to the families who join us, but one of the most important is help with home repair. For us it is a question of health. Families will not prosper if every rain soaks them. So we give them tin roofing, nails, some cement, and a small stipend that they can use to pay a builder. They must provide the lumber, rocks, sand, water, and other building materials the home requires.

Mirlène's tin roof was still in place, but the door had been removed, as had the more valuable lumber. The walls, built up of rocks and mud, were starting to collapse in places where support poles had been taken away. The yard around it was unswept, cluttered with leaves, straw, pebbles, and other debris.

Shortly before I got to the house, I had passed a group of farmers, barefoot young men wearing ragged t-shirts and torn jeans, clearing a small field. They were preparing the soil for planting, lifting their hoes up more or less in unison, then bringing them down on the earth, chatting a patter of jokes and gossip to shorten the day's work.

I returned to ask them what had happened. One of them was Orélès's brother, and he told me that I would find the couple at the home of a *medsen fèy*, or "leaf doctor," a practitioner of traditional forms of healing, who lived a short walk farther to the east.

In an area like Bwawouj, a long and difficult hike from the nearest doctor or nurse, people still depend on men and women with advanced knowledge of herbs, essential oils and massage. *Medsen fèy* sometimes use incantations or other religious practices as well. The *medsen's* house was on the edge of a *lakou* of four or five small huts. I knew I'd found it when I saw the colorful flags that mark the *lakou* as belonging to a practitioner of *vodoun*.

His was the largest of the huts, though made of woven sticks just as the others were. Its tin roof and the care that had been taken to decorate it were all that set it apart. The smoothed-over mud that covered its walls had been painted blue and white, and there were designs painted onto it in pinkish red. The smaller, undecorated huts that surrounded it made the *lakou* into a kind of inpatient clinic, where sick followers could come to stay while receiving treatment. When I got to the healer's house, his wife sent me to another smaller one at the other end of a short footpath.

Mirlène had been near death during the last months of the program. She and their second child, a baby just a few months old, had grown sick with fever and diarrhea at the same time. Orélès rushed to the midwife who had delivered their child, afraid that the girl was dying because he hadn't yet paid the bill. The midwife took his money and said, *"Dlo a gaye. Veye kanari a."* That means, "The water has spilled. Look after the pitcher." She was telling him that he wouldn't be able to save his little girl and that he should focus on saving his wife instead. So he ran back home. By the time he got there, the infant was dead.

But he was able to get Mirlène the help she needed to pull through, taking her to another *medsen fèy* across the mountains, near Bouli. After a few weeks of rest and treatment, she had recovered and was able to graduate from the program.

Now it was his turn to be sick. Orélès had been in bed for over a week, unable to do anything for himself.

I followed the footpath that I had been directed toward, and found myself in a small yard between two houses. The larger was on my left, a two-room house built of stone and mud, covered with a roof of rusted tin. On the right, opposite a small grassy slope, was a tiny one-room hut. A fire burned on the ground in front of it between three small rocks. The pot that sat on the rocks was starting to boil. The hut's walls were built of woven palm leaves and its roof was made of *tach*.

I ducked inside the hut, bending deeply to avoid hitting my head on the low, rough-hewn rafters. Then I sat on the edge of a bed that took up nearly the whole house. There was no other furniture. Orélès was lying on his side, facing toward me. He smiled weakly as I greeted him. He couldn't sit up, but insisted on taking the time to ask about my health and the health of my family. I rested my hand on the back of his neck, thin but muscular from the loads he was accustomed to carrying on his head, and I could feel the heat of the fever that was making his joints ache.

I had met Orélès as a short, slim, but powerfully built man, with the arm strength that comes from farming and the leg strength that comes from growing up at the very top of a steep, 5,500-foot hill. But he was curled up on the hard wooden bed with his light brown face resting uncomfortably on the cloth sack filled with old clothes that counted as a pillow. He spoke about how hard things had been the last days. He was most anxious to make me understand that he'd been so sick that others had to feed him and clean him up when he went to the bathroom on himself. He repeated that several times, that he had been going to the bathroom on himself, as though that was the key to making me understand his misery.

He was starting to feel better, he said, but was not yet able to get out of bed. Both he and his wife believed that his sickness was directly connected to the plot of land where they had built their new house. That is why they had decided to abandon it. Their land was cursed.

He and Mirlène had lost a child, and then Mirlène had been on the point of death. Now Oréles was sick. And their problems had started shortly after they moved into their new home. For Haitians in the countryside, the timing, with one serious illness following quickly upon another, was such that seeing the land as cursed was a simple matter of putting two and two together.

But now that Oréles was starting to feel better, the couple already had a plan. They would tear down the house and rebuild it on another plot, which his brother had promised to give them. Their surviving daughter was staying with Mirlène's mother, so they only had each other to look after, and they both said they were determined to face their future together. They hadn't sold off any livestock yet, so they had resources enough for a new beginning. If Oréles recovered quickly, he would even be able to help Mirlène get their bean crop into the ground in time for the rainy season, and a decent harvest would put them back on their feet again. As things stood, Mirlène's hard work and help from Oréles's brother and sister-in-law were ensuring that they were eating reasonably well. Despite everything, the couple seemed hopeful. And I was hopeful, too.

I still had a long hike ahead of me, down from Bwawouj along the twisting path that zigzags gradually into the Regalis valley, then along the riverbed and up into Kochon Mawon, in the hills that separate Regalis from Thomonde, and finally back down through Boukan Leyona into Bay Tourib. It would take another couple of hours. By the time I'd arrive at the residence, it would be getting dark.

Hiking alone through the mountains of central Haiti, I'd have time to think. This was the third time I had made the trip between Bay Tourib and Zaboka. I had been part of the CLM team for almost three years, and we were now preparing graduation for the second group of families that I'd been closely involved with. The women had started out poorer than anyone I had ever imagined, unable to feed themselves and their children even a single meal every day. Not because they had been overwhelmed by famine or drought or any other natural disaster, but because they were simply that poor. Yet almost all of them had changed their lives during the time that they spent with us.

Their transformations were unfolding, however, in ways that I had not foreseen. Much of our program is built to look like a straightforward procedure. We carefully select the families that will participate and then accompany the women who lead those families through a series of particular steps, offering specific forms of support. It would be easy to imagine that a simple explanation of the steps we lead them through would enable one to understand what we do.

But it would not. Because each woman's success is tied to the unique way she learns to live her life. We call the program "the Pathway to a Better Life," but the name is misleading in one respect. There is no single such path. And we would not succeed if we pretended that there was one. One can only understand the pathway out of poverty by meeting the women who make the journey with us, and considering how their individual stories unfold.

Ytelet and Dieulonet, with their little sister
Dieumanette in the middle

⇒ 19 ⇐

Martinière and Ytelet

Martinière arrived in Zaboka early Sunday afternoon to get ready for his week of home visits. When he got there, he found Dorsilia in a panic. She had been waiting for him since early in the day. Her neighbor Ytelet was dying, and nobody wanted to do anything about it.

Martinière put down his backpack and ran off with Dorsilia. They found Ytelet lying in her small hut with a very high fever. She was terribly weak. So was her little brother, Dieulonet, who lives with her.

The case managers hadn't visited Zaboka the previous week. They had been in another part of Boucan Carré, at a training session for members there. And there's no easy way for them to get news of what's happening in Zaboka between visits. Few locals have cell phones because points where you can get any reception are few and far between. Apparently Ytelet and Dieulonet had been deteriorating for days. Martinière asked her family why they hadn't led them to the hospital, and they answered that they didn't have the kind of sickness a hospital could treat.

This is a common perspective in rural Haiti. There are sicknesses that are considered "*maladi doktè*" or "doctor's sicknesses," and those that are not. Ytelet's family had spoken to local healers, who told them she was going to die. They couldn't see the point in carrying her all the way down the mountain to the hospital just to have to carry her corpse back up for burial.

When Martinière learned that Ytelet's family had no thought of bringing her to the hospital, he made a lot of noise, but he couldn't convince them to take responsibility to get her and her brother the care they needed. They couldn't understand why an outsider like Martinière was so excited by Ytelet's situation. They liked Martinière. But they were, they said, "used to death."

So Martinière thought of our team instead. He had already made the long hike up to Zaboka, but he decided to run up the steep, treacherous path from Zaboka to Belepe to get a telephone signal. He called our driver, Wilfaut, who was at home in Léogâne, about five hours away. Wilfaut was spending Sunday with his wife and kids, but he immediately got into our four-door pickup truck and started on his way. Martinière called me next. I was already on my way down to Port au Prince from my home in the mountains above Pétion-Ville. Once I was in the loop, I was able to communicate with Wilfaut, who agreed to pick me up on his way through Port au Prince. We planned to meet Martinière, Ytelet, and Dieulonet in Feyobyen, the market at the end of the road that cuts through Boucan Carré. This would cut a final hour out of their long hike to the hospital.

Martinière then went back down the hill into Zaboka, grabbed a stretcher from Nava's house, unfolded it in front of Ytelet's home, and recruited a program member's husband to help him carry Ytelet down to the hospital. Ashamed of the effort that Martinière was making to save his daughter, her father Sourit agreed to carry his son Dieulonet on his shoulders. He would walk down the hill with a neighbor, another member's husband, and they'd take turns carrying the boy.

The road from the main highway into Boucan Carré was in bad shape at the time. Stretches of deep, muddy ruts alternated with loose stones all the way to the hospital near Chanbo. From Chanbo to Feyobyen things only got worse. The road twisted narrowly through the mud, between fields of corn and beans planted along the Boucan Carré River. Fording two major streams and the deep mud that filled the remnants of a third, Wilfaut picked his way through and around the ruts, carefully choosing between the ones to avoid and the ones to take with enough speed that his truck's momentum could carry us through.

We met up with Martinière and the rest just before we got to Feyobyen. Dorsilia and Clemancia had come down with the men. They climbed into the back of the truck with Martinière, and we put Ytelet and Dieulonet in the back seat. The men turned around and headed straight back to Zaboka.

Ytelet and Dieulonet were in terrible shape when we got them to the hospital: fevered, dehydrated and terribly hungry. I took Dieulonet in my arms to carry him inside, while Martinière and the women helped Ytelet.

I am not a big, strong man. I sometimes think I look as though I was drawn as a stick figure. But Dieulonet weighed nothing. I was shocked at how easily I swept a boy almost in his teens into my arms, and carried him in. There was nothing left of him. I laid him on a table, in front of the admissions office, and the Partners in Health staff quickly found a bed for him in the maternity ward.

I ran out to the street in front of the hospital to buy the first calories I could find. They were crackers. When I got them in front of Dieulonet, he began to reach for them with his lips even before I could get them out of their cellophane wrapper. He was desperately hungry.

The hospital staff was initially resigned to the unfortunate fact that they had no bed available for Ytelet, but resignation is not one of Martinière's strengths. He stood in the middle of the hospital courtyard, screaming at people until the nurses had to change their minds.

Having gotten Ytelet and Dieulonet settled, Martinière gave Dorsilia and Clemancia some money. They had come down the mountain to attend to Ytelet and Dieulonet. The hospital's care would be free of charge, and the patients would be fed, but Dorsilia and Clemancia would need to eat as well. Patients in Haitian hospitals typically depend on family members for some aspects of their care. Haitian nurses don't usually feed or wash patients, or clean up after them. So having someone who stays with you is important, even in a hospital run by Partners in Health.

After ensuring that they were all set, Martinière hiked back up to Zaboka to work the next day. When he got there, it was long past dark. He crossed paths with a group of laborers relaxing after a hard day's work in the field. They said that they hoped it would be as easy for him to carry Ytelet back up the hill as it had been to carry her down. In other words, they did not expect her to recover. They thought he'd have to return her to Zaboka for burial. They added that they looked forward to the coffee and bread. It had been a long time since they'd had any. Coffee and bread is typical fare for a rural Haitian wake.

But both Ytelet and Dieulonet recovered. Ytelet was out of the hospital within a couple of days. Then she stuck around to take over care of her little brother. Dieulonet was ready to leave shortly after that.

I don't have access to medical records. I'm not sure just what Ytelet and Dieulonet had. But as sick as they seemed, they were both ready to make the long hike back to Zaboka within a week. They seemed to be at death's door. Even years later, Martinière and I sometimes talk about the sight of Dieulonet reaching for crackers with his lips. Yet they were both strikingly savable. But no one was willing to make the effort it took to save them.

"If it wasn't for Martinière, I wouldn't be here," Ytelet says. "Neither would Dieulonet. We would be dead. When Martinière stood up in the hospital yelling at everyone, it was a really big deal. Now my family sees that I matter."

≥ 20 ≤

Franck Laurore

The chapel in Piton was badly damaged by the earthquake of January 12, 2010. When we visited later that summer, about a third of the back wall remained, just a triangle of cinder blocks covering the lower left-hand corner. As you looked behind the pulpit, you could see a plantain grove and fruit trees through the empty space where the wall once stood. The chapel's support posts were mostly in place. The poured concrete was cracked in places and the rebar that strengthens them was slightly bent, but they continued to hold up the tin roof. The other walls, though they showed numerous cracks, still stood mostly intact. But sitting within the chapel you felt as though you were in a ruin.

Piton is part of Fondwa, a rural community in the mountains between Port au Prince and Jacmel, about four hours away from the region where we do our work. Our team went there to attend a funeral. Franck Laurore, one of our new case managers, was killed on the job.

Laurore was part of a team of four who had been assigned to collect data in Tifon, on the far side of the lake in Pelig that was formed when a hydroelectric dam was built decades ago. The team had been working in Tifon for several days. They were following up community meetings, identifying the families who might qualify for our help.

Each day, three of them would take a canoe-ferry over and back across the lake while Laurore would walk. The extra hike would take him over an hour each way, but Laurore couldn't swim, so he was scared of the boats. Most of them are dugout canoes that no reasonable person would believe in.

The people from Tifon use the canoes because that's what's available, unless you are willing to walk. And if you have a sack or two of charcoal or produce to bring to market in Domon, Difayi or Mirebalais, hiking isn't really an option.

All across Haiti, people generally just accept transportation that is some combination of dangerous and uncomfortable. Cheap Chinese motorcycles carry three or four passengers lined up tightly behind a driver. A child or two might sit in front as well. Produce and charcoal trucks roll into Port au Prince from the countryside with crowds of market women and others perched high on top of the piled-up sacks. And there are the ubiquitous tap-taps, colorfully painted pickup trucks in various degrees of disrepair that have benches in the back. They carry 15 to 20 adults or more. All these vehicles tend to be poorly maintained, and their drivers take chances on roads that are mostly narrow and curved, even if they are paved.

But Laurore chose to walk. It was a lot of extra effort on top of hard fieldwork every day, but he was simply afraid. Growing up in Piton, he would have been a long way from any place where he might have learned to swim.

At the end of his last day of work, however, Laurore was exhausted. The team had been hiking all day up and down Tifon's steep hills. They had run out of drinking water and had nothing to eat. When they got back to the lake late in the afternoon, the other case managers were surprised to see him negotiating the price of the crossing with the oarsman. He was just too tired for the extra walk.

The canoe got most of the way across the lake when a freak storm appeared. Its high winds quickly swamped the boat. Two of the team members were able to swim to safety. Seraphin, who cannot swim, was saved because the wind had blown the canoe so close to the dam that a bystander was able to climb down and throw him a cloth to grab hold of. Laurore panicked and went straight to the bottom. The last thing his team heard him say was, "*Gade jan m ap mouri!*" "Look how I'm dying!" A group of local men dove after his body, but it had sunk too deep. It reappeared two days later, when it floated to the surface, just a few feet from the dam.

Laurore was 29, his aging parents' sixth and youngest child. Members of our team met with his older sister and her husband to plan the funeral. He had lived with them throughout his high school years in Port au Prince, sent to school in the capital like many promising rural kids, because his family thought it was the best way to invest in his future.

His sister and brother-in-law had lots of understandable questions about their little brother's death, but the most striking thing about the meeting was their very vocal determination that Laurore's work continue. Even in his first months with the team he had apparently told them enough about what we do, enough about the desperate poverty of those we serve, to convince them of the work's importance.

Laurore had originally applied for a job as a credit agent at Fonkoze's branch office in Fondwa. Jobs are hard to come by in Haiti. The country's unemployment rate is said to be over 40%. A credit agent's salary isn't great. They make less than $200 per month. But it is a reliable paycheck, something very few Haitian adults have. An extremely rural area like Fondwa would likely have almost no formal jobs at all. So he and his family must have been disappointed when he didn't get the one at Fonkoze.

But the team that was selecting families for the original *Chemen Lavi Miyò* pilot needed help. There were too few case managers to get the job done quickly. They found Laurore's resumé at our central office, interviewed him, and offered him the job. He joined the team, and then continued as a credit agent in the Central Plateau. It was a long way from home, but it was work. When Fonkoze received funding to scale up *Chemen Lavi Miyò*, he was one of the first case managers we hired. It was a big promotion. His salary doubled.

In planning our participation at his funeral, we had chosen one of his fellow case managers to give a short speech on our behalf, telling how much Laurore had meant to us. Then one of his friends got up to give a second eulogy. He said little about Laurore, however. He was angry, and he used his moment on the pulpit to tell the assembled that Fonkoze had killed his closest friend. If we had given Laurore the job in Fondwa that he first wanted, he would still be alive.

It was a terrible moment that just went on and on. The young man couldn't seem to find enough bad things to say about us.

Finally, he finished and Laurore's father stepped up to speak. He thanked everyone for coming. There wasn't much that he could do to take the sting out of the young man's bitter words. But he asked us to make sure that Laurore's work does not stop.

And the work is continuing. Two days after the funeral, all the teams but Laurore's were back in the field. Two of that team's three surviving members were still too shocked to work, but the other was studying the remains of their soaked-through documents to determine what of their data could be salvaged and what would have to be collected all over again.

Our staff was badly shaken. But their determination kept them on the job.

As I sat at the funeral with César, another of the new case managers, he explained this well. He talked to me about a woman he had met on the previous Tuesday, pregnant and living alone with three children and nowhere to sleep but a straw mat on the floor of her open little hut. She had found nothing to feed her kids that morning and wasn't sure what she would give them the rest of the day. "When you see the way a woman like her is forced to live," he said, "it's easy to keep your mind on the job you need to do."

⇒ 21 ⇐

Rose Marthe and Cholera

It was Sunday afternoon, and we had just arrived in Zaboka for our regular visit when someone told us that Rose Marthe had been rushed to the cholera treatment center there. We hurried back down from our base at Nava's house to the stream that snakes through Zaboka. It splits the village in two and also serves as its main path. In winter and early spring, it dries to a trickle. But as the rainy season commences in late spring, it starts to rise, and you just have to resign yourself to wading through it.

We splashed through ankle-deep water as we hurried down the rocky, sandy bed until we got to the path that leads up toward Dieupanou's *lakou*. We were anxious to see Rose Marthe immediately.

Dieupanou had learned how to treat cholera while working as an employee of World Vision down in lower Boucan Carré. As the number of cases around his home in Zaboka started to mount, he saw a business opportunity. He set up his own fee-for-service center, using materials that he would buy in regular trips with his mule down to Mirebalais. He was off in Mirebalais when we arrived, so there was no one in the center who had any real training. But he had shown his wife how to change an IV, and she was keeping an eye on each of the patients, making sure none of their IVs ran out.

Cholera is a nasty disease. It causes such violent vomiting and diarrhea that many of its victims die before they can get help. It's especially dangerous in areas like Wòch Djèp, where Rose Marthe lives. The nearest health care is hours away on foot, the only transportation that's available. And victims of sudden and severe dehydration are in no condition to hike anywhere at all. During the first months of the outbreak, we would encounter men carrying the stricken on stretchers, taking them down the long mountain footpaths that crisscross northern Boucan Carré. The stretchers were usually jury-rigged arrangements of rough wooden poles and *tach*. The bearers would try to improvise something tent-like above the victim's face, as protection from the tropical sun.

We'd also come across abandoned stretchers, left on the side of the path wherever the bearers had discovered that the trip to the hospital no longer served any purpose. A shallow grave was sure to be nearby. People wouldn't want to risk moving a corpse that might infect those around it.

Rose Marthe's husband, Sepavre, could have taken her to the free Partners in Health cholera center in Central Boucan Carré rather than to the fee-for-service center in Zaboka. But his choice was complicated. The care at the Partners in Health center would have been free, but Sepavre would have needed to stay with Rose Marthe. Neither had family near the center, and Haitians at inpatient clinics need a family member to help them with basic needs that Haitian hospital staffs do not take on. But he and his wife had a house full of young children to think about. If he were to stay with Rose Marthe, they'd have no one to look after the kids.

He had family in Zaboka, though. So once he got Rose Marthe to Zaboka, he could go home to look after the kids. He'd leave Rose Marthe in his family's hands.

We found her at Dieupanou's center, lying on a straw mat, much as she had been lying on one when I visited her at her home days after her youngest child had been born. The mat was spread out on the ground under Dieupanou's *kolonbi*, the small hut built on stilts that families in the Central Plateau use to store their harvests. A *kolonbi* sits on its four corner posts, and its builder wraps each post with a band of roofing tin. Rats' claws can't grip the tin, so they can't get up the posts to the stored grain.

The space underneath the *kolonbi* had been turned into an additional room, enclosed with sheets that Dieupanou had hung from the *kolonbi*'s raised floor and tied to its legs. He had set up an IV by hanging it from a nail that had been driven into one of the *kolonbi*'s twisted wooden support posts.

Rose Marthe looked awful, huddled on a dirty straw mat beneath a thin sheet. The fluids she had received hadn't yet brought her back to life.

At first she didn't want to look at us. She kept her body turned toward the sheet that served as a wall. She was afraid that we'd be angry, because she had recovered enough of her senses to recognize that she couldn't have gotten sick if she hadn't been careless. And Martinière is not a quiet soul. When he is angry, he lets you know it.

But Rose Marthe started to relax when she saw that none of Martinière's plentiful anger was for her. He couldn't believe that Dieupanou's people had left her lying on the ground, without even a bed, and he started to ask loud, pointed questions. How could they leave a desperately sick woman lying on the ground? Weren't they ashamed of themselves? She was eventually going to have to pay them for all the care she was receiving, pay them with money that she could barely afford, and they couldn't even find her a bed?

He's no diplomat. Madan Dieupanou tried to calm him down, asking him just to wait until Dieupanou got back. But Martinière is neither calm nor patient when something important is at stake, and he was starting making lots of noise. So she set up a bed in one of the *lakou*'s empty huts, and we moved Rose Marthe into it.

She was still weak as we headed back to our base. But as we left, we could see her starting to smile in the little light that the gathering twilight provided. We went back to see her every afternoon during the couple of days we spent in Zaboka, but on Wednesday morning we had to leave Zaboka to work in other communities, including Wòch Djèp, so we wouldn't have news of Rose Marthe until the following week.

When we got back up to Zaboka, Rose Marthe had left the center to return home. She had stayed in that abandoned hut, taking first IVs and then oral fluids, for another six days. But once she recovered her strength, she took the long walk back to Sepavre and their children across the hills in Wòch Djèp.

Chiver and Memène

⇒ 22 ⇐

Memène and Chiver

I went to the beauty salon with two case managers, Christian and Sandra. It wasn't anywhere I could have expected to be. I don't go to such places. I wouldn't normally have reason to. My gray, buzz-cut hair doesn't really call for styling, and I chew my fingernails too obsessively to require a manicure.

We had gone to ask for help for a woman Christian was working with. Memène lives in Demare, a farming community behind the Labasti market in southern Mirebalais. Her relationship with her partner Chiver had been an issue for Christian and me for several months, and we had not gotten very far.

They are a young couple. Memène is 22, and Chiver just a few years older than that. They live with two children, Memène's daughter and Chiver's son. They don't yet have a child together. When we met them, they were living in a very dilapidated shack with a roof of dried, cracked *tach* on a plot of land that belongs to Bossiquot, Chiver's father. The *lakou* lies along a dirt road that leads off the main highway behind the Labasti market into Demare, on a slope that sinks steeply below the dirt road. Further down the slope is the front end of a cane field that belongs to a much wealthier family. The ox-powered mill that squeezes the juice out the cane is just across a small ravine, right next to the large straw tent that covers the cauldron where the juice is boiled into syrup. Bossiquot's *lakou* includes several equally dilapidated homes on it, including Bossiqout's, and more than one of the households qualified for our program. It is an especially poor little cluster of families, and Christian was working with them all.

Early on in our engagement with the couple, we heard reports of violence. Chiver was beating Memène. Tikomè, another member who lives just down the path from them, had pulled Christian aside. She asked him to do something. "*L ap tiye l.*" "He'll kill her," she said.

Christian rushed to meet with Memène, and she explained to him how Chiver ended up losing his temper most recently. It wasn't the first time he had hit her. Christian spoke with Chiver as well. After some conversation, Memène decided to leave Chiver. She'd move back in with her mother, who is also a member of the program and lives close by, just on the other side of the Labasti market. It seemed like the obvious thing to do. The two women would be able to build their houses next to each other on the mother's land.

But Memène didn't want Chiver prosecuted. Maybe it was because it was prison that had separated her from her daughter's father. Maybe she was afraid of what Chiver might do if he was arrested but wasn't sent to jail. We were sorry that she wasn't willing to press charges, but we couldn't force the issue. Christian planned the move with them both, and Chiver agreed to turn over the livestock we had given her, which had been in his care.

Christian went by a few days later and found Memène back in the house with Chiver. Christian is a soft-spoken man with a deliberate manner. He's just over six feet tall, so he towers over almost all of the women we work with, and over their husbands and partners as well. When he does his rounds of home visits, he carries his motorcycle helmet with him as a makeshift chair. He's unflappable, and one of the keys to his success has been the easy and patient manner he shows as members share their problems with him.

He talked to Memène and Chiver separately and made sure that she really wanted to be back with Chiver. That was about all that he could do. She affirmed her decision, so he talked to Chiver about how important it was that the violence stop. Christian asked me to talk to them, too.

I went by the next day, and we had a long conversation. I asked them to explain what their problem was. I had a hard time following the argument between them as they got angrier and angrier, but despite all the yelling I got the impression that they really did want to stay together. The most striking thing was that Memène was less interested in talking about what Chiver had done to her than about the way he sticks up for her when she argues with his mother and sisters.

Chiver, for his part, kept insisting that Memène could go if she wanted to, but he was close to tears. You could tell he didn't really mean it.

When I told Chiver that hitting his wife could get him arrested, he started talking about all the things she does to make him lose his temper. Some of those things would have made me mad, too.

I do not blame the victim. All the violence is entirely his fault. She doesn't force him to hit her. Memène does however say some very mean things. In front of us, she is much quieter than he is. But she is much better with words. When she says something mean, he doesn't know how to answer.

But I cut him off in the middle of his explanation. I had to. I put my left arm around his shoulder to draw him close and took his left hand in my right. I wanted to ensure that I had his full attention and I wanted him to feel that my intentions were friendly.

"Listen, Chiver. I know she says things to make you mad. But if you tell a judge you hit her because of something she said, he will not listen. He'll send you to jail."

"But she called me a thief," he cried.

"It doesn't matter. Before you hit her, she could be wrong and so could you. Once you hit her, you're the one who's wrong."

And I added that he didn't need to take my word for it. He could ask any of his friends or neighbors.

One of the members of our Village Assistance Committee was there, a man not much older than Chiver, and he chimed in: "*Se sa li ye.*" "That's the way it is."

I tried to keep my tone friendly but clear. I needed him to feel prison as a threat. But as long as Memène chose to stay with him, I couldn't let him think of Christian and me as his enemies. She and the children would be better off if he continued to work with us. I was inclined to think that she should get out of the house, but it had to be her decision, and she wasn't making it.

The peace we established that day held up for almost six weeks. And the couple accomplished a lot during that time. Chiver added a pig to what we had given them with money he was paid for driving the oxen that milled his neighbor's cane. They also installed their latrine, put the tin roof on their house, and began to build up their wealth by taking very good care of their livestock. I went by once a week or so just to check in and to see how they were doing, and I always got friendly greetings from both.

They are a handsome pair. Memène is a small, slight woman with big, pronounced cheekbones and small eyes. Chiver seems short to me, but he towers over her. His shoulders are broad and he's very muscular, with big eyes and an easy smile. When we first met him, he was letting his hair grow out into short dreadlocks that would stand up on his head. Christian is a very conservative Protestant, however, and he somehow convinced Chiver to cut his hair and keep it short.

Memène and Chiver were still arguing frequently, but Chiver would call Christian whenever he started to lose his temper. He knows he is hotheaded, and he seems to want to change. Christian would go help them talk things through. Their relationship was becoming a big part of his job. Two or three times, Memène and Chiver decided to split up, and Christian would help them plan the steps of a clean separation. Then after a day or two, he would find them together again.

But one day, Memène told Christian that Chiver had once again hit and kicked her. This time, she said she really wanted to leave him. Christian talked with them to arrange the separation because he wanted to ensure both that Memène would feel safe and that she would keep the assets we had helped her build.

By this point things had gotten a little complicated. The little wealth they had begun to accumulate was too intertwined to separate easily. For example, the couple had built their house by putting Memène's tin roofing on a structure that belonged to Chiver, on his father's land. They had also used money we supplied to pay the builders who installed the roof and built up the stone walls that took the place of the original ones, which were woven of sticks. We couldn't get the builder's fee back. It had been paid. But Christian and Chiver calculated how much Chiver would have to pay Memène if he kept the roofing material, and he agreed to the sum. It would be more sensible than removing the roof and returning the material to her. Chiver and Christian even created a realistic payment plan. We thought we had things worked out, but then Memène decided, once more, to return.

This only proved that Christian and I were in over our heads, that we didn't know how to help Memène. And it's why we went to the beauty parlor. Its owner and head beautician is Minouche. She works for the Haitian government ministry that is especially charged with the affairs of women, the *Ministère des Conditions Féminines*. We needed both expertise and clout, and we went to Minouche hoping that she'd be able to provide them.

We sat in the parlor as we talked, on plastic chairs which would normally be filled with women getting manicures, pedicures, or having their hair done. Shelves were filled with brightly colored bottles and jars of lotions and creams. Brushes and combs of different shapes and sizes were arranged on tables that ran along the walls.

I asked Minouche to turn down the radio. When Haitians come to a barbershop or beauty parlor, they expect music and they want it to be loud. But she understood my need for quiet, so she had the young woman who cleans and sweeps to turn down the radio before she sent her outside. Then Minouche settled in and prepared to listen. When she had heard our explanations, she said that she'd be happy to help out. She'd been told about our work, had been admiring it from a distance, and was glad to contribute.

That was Sunday evening, and Christian made sure that Memène and Chiver would be at home the following Tuesday afternoon. We picked up Minouche at her beauty parlor, just around the corner from our office, and brought her to Demare in our pickup truck.

We stepped into the small space in front of the couple's house, and they offered Minouche a chair. She began by introducing herself, her office and her role. She was there, she said, neither for Memène nor for Chiver. Her job was to help them both solve the problems they had with each other. If the solution was separation, she would help them through that process step by step, guaranteeing that Memène would get all the protection she needed. If the couple wanted to stay together, she would help them figure what each of them would need to do to make that work. She closed her little introduction with a threat: She stared straight at Chiver as she added, "But if I decide to have you arrested, there's nowhere you can hide."

Chiver started angrily, resentful because we had called in authorities, but his anger passed even before he finished his first set of explanations. He's an emotional man, and can get heated quickly once he starts talking. He made a long story of the way the latest fight started.

Memène had gone to her mother's house for a small *vodoun* celebration. For several days in a row, she would disappear early in the morning, telling Chiver nothing. She wouldn't come back until late in the afternoon. Their home was in disarray, he said. The children and their clothes were dirty because she was more worried about the celebration than about her own home. He was out every day, in fields, in mills, or wherever he could find a little work. He needed her to take care of the house and the kids.

His frustration had been building. The last straw came when he went to the market to buy some pig feed. He was hungry, so he also bought a meal and sat down to enjoy it right there. Memène saw him, and was angry because he was eating out of the home. Neighbors would see him eating in the market, and they might think that she didn't take care of her man. Chiver had called Memène over to share his meal with him, but she said they had food at home. He tried to convince her, but it just made her madder. She said that if he was going to eat out, he better not eat at home at all.

When he got home, they starting yelling right away.

"Memène, I took you in naked off the street because your husband was a thief," Chiver said.

She answered that the man was innocent, then she added that "there are thieves who act in a bottle of clear glass, and others who hide their deeds in a black bottle instead." Chiver was, she implied, the one who deserved jail, but he hadn't yet been caught.

She was once again calling him a thief.

Chiver and I were sitting next to one another in the dirt in front of the house as he explained. He was getting more and more animated as the story went on. He kept starting to stand, but I would put my hand on his shoulder, asking him to calm down. We would listen to everything he wanted to say. Minouche and Memène were sitting in the couple's two small chairs.

He finally got to the moment when they started to fight. Chiver showed me a mark above his eye that he claimed Memène made by hitting him with their broom. He had grabbed her by the throat, he said, to push her away.

Minouche listened to the whole story, but when Chiver seemed finished and it was her turn to speak, she went directly to the point:

"Do you want her to stay with you so you can spend your lives together?"

Chiver first avoided the question: "*Li mèt fè sa l vle.*" "She can do whatever she wants."

"*Se pa sa m te di w,*" Minouche answered. "That's not what I asked you. I asked you what you want."

Minouche really pushed him, and he was in tears when he said that he wanted her to stay: "She's the one who wants to leave. I didn't ask her to go away."

When Minouche asked Chiver what Memène would have to change for him to feel as though he could make their partnership work, he said that the only thing about her that he could not accept is that she leaves the house for hours at a time without letting him or anyone else know where she is going. "*Se sa sèlman*," he repeated several times. "That's the only thing."

Minouche agreed that neither husband nor wife should wander off without letting the other one know.

She now asked Memène to speak, and this is when her work started to get difficult. Memène has trouble even looking at people she isn't used to, let alone talking to them. But Minouche persisted.

Memène admitted that she had called Chiver a thief, but he had made her really mad. He pushed her, and then she grabbed the broom to try to defend herself. He had grabbed her by the throat and pushed her down onto their bed, and when she got up he kicked her in the chest.

Minouche got to the point again:

"Do you want to stay with Chiver or do you want to leave?"

"I won't stay."

Asked to explain, she said that he kept hitting her. Minouche then asked her whether, if we could change that about him, she would want to stay with him. And she said that she did.

This took some persuasion on Minouche's part. Minouche seemed to have decided from the start that staying together would probably be best for Memène if we could make it safe for her to do so. She talked about Chiver's good qualities. He was ready to work hard to support her and her children. Memène readily agreed to that much. Minouche pointed out how easily Memène could end up with a partner who was much worse, always repeating, however, that Chiver would have to stop hitting her.

Talking to Memène took a lot of time. She was reluctant to speak, and Chiver kept cutting her off. The more he defended himself, the more heated he became. And as he became more heated and louder, a crowd of neighbors began to gather, ready to enjoy the spectacle. Minouche started to get frustrated, put off by the regular interruptions that our spectators' laughter and commentary produced, so she had us move into the one-room house.

There is no space for chairs inside, but there are two beds, a larger one for the two adults and a much smaller one for their two kids. We sat on the beds, knee to knee, and continued to talk.

The more we talked, the more Minouche and I learned about issues beyond what Memène and Chiver were initially willing to admit. On Chiver's side, the most serious thing was that Memène was always hurting his feelings with things she would say. He didn't put things that way, but he didn't need to. He was on the verge of tears several times as he talked of things she had said that had cut him to the quick. On Memène's side, she talked more and more of her little girl. Though Chiver repeatedly said he had two children in the home – his son and Memène's daughter – and that they both felt like his, Memène complained that he didn't treat them equally. She said that when he's angry he uses terribly ugly words to yell at her girl.

Minouche had succeeded at getting to a deeper layer of the couple's conflict, so she asked them each once more, at this more serious level, whether they wanted to spend their lives with each other. Chiver didn't hesitate this time. But Memène had a hard time answering. Here I interrupted to ask her and Minouche whether it might be better if Chiver and I left so that they could talk privately, woman to woman. Minouche thanked me, and so I led Chiver back out of the house.

I asked him to take me down to look at their pigs. We followed the narrow footpath that leads down from the road, past his front door, and then to the small grove of mangos and avocados farther below. He had chosen a shady spot among the trees to build a small pen out of knee-high corner posts and planks cut of palm wood. The couple's pigs were tied up inside. The one Chiver had purchased had an injured foot, which looked like it was starting to get infected. The pig was limping, and one of its front hooves seemed swollen. Christian and I had come without medications, so I told him I'd have Christian come treat the foot the next day.

When Minouche called us back in, she said that Memène had decided to stay with Chiver. She explained that she would create an agreement between them, specifying the conditions each would have to respect in order to make their relationship work. They each would sign the agreement and she would file it in her office and in the courthouse in Mirebalais. Writing the agreement took some time. It was getting dark as we got in the truck to head back to Mirebalais.

As we left, I gave Chiver a long hug. It gave me a way to whisper into his ear. I needed to say something to him alone. I told him that I hoped he wasn't angry that we had brought the government down on him, but that we had to protect his wife. We had acted in the hope that it would be good for both of them. As he said that he understood, he returned the pressure of my embrace. He said he was glad that we had come.

Then I went to Memène. She's much shorter than I am, so I had to bend down to kiss the crown of her head. I told her to remember that we were on her side. As long as she chose to stay with Chiver, we would do what we could to help her live with him, but that if she ever decided to leave, we would help her do that too. She smiled as I straightened up to walk back to the waiting truck.

I learned to make visits to Memène and Chiver a regular part of my week. I would rarely find Chiver early in the day. He would be in the fields. But I could see Memène and hear about her side of things. If I went in the late afternoon, I could see them both and get a good sense of the progress they were making.

And they were progressing very quickly, more quickly than almost anyone we worked with. At least economically. Memène had a small, steady income. It had started with the weekly stipend that we were providing, but Christian had also taught her to manage a little business, and she was doing a good job. She was selling basic groceries – rice, cooking oil, sugar, and the like – out of her home, and was keeping the household more or less fed by herself, even after we stopped providing the stipend.

And because the family could now depend on her, rather than on Chiver's daily contribution, he started to make money hand over foot. He is one of the most sought-after farm workers in the area, and rich neighbors were willing to pay him well to do major jobs in their fields. Instead of a day's work for about $1, he would get contracts for 100 or even 200 times as much to harvest a whole field of cane or weed a garden of corn or beans.

I was at a workshop we held for women in Demare and Labasti about 14 months into the program. Gauthier was visiting, and he was listening to women as they stood up to talk about the progress they had made thus far. The women were seated, crowded onto long plank benches that had been organized in a square. I saw Memène sitting across the room, staring down at her feet as others spoke. So I waited for my chance and I asked her to stand up and tell Gauthier about herself.

It took some prodding, but she finally started to talk. "My name is Memène. My husband and I started with nothing. Now I have a house with a latrine. I have pigs and goats. My husband bought me a cow with money we made with my animals, then he bought two more with money from jobs he did. He works really hard." For all they had been through together, she was proud enough of her husband to brag about him.

But her pride didn't make their partnership any less volatile. A few weeks later, I was sitting in their house with the two of them, as they screamed at each other. "The only reason I need a woman is to take care of my boy," Chiver complained. He explained that he had come home the previous afternoon to find his boy covered in dust. "She won't even bathe the boy while I'm out in the fields."

"It's not true. I bathed him. But there's so much dust. The kids don't stay clean."

"Steve," he told me, "I know I can't hit her anymore, but as soon as she graduates, she should just go back to her mother's house. I'll find another woman who'll take care of my son."

And two more weeks after that, I found them happy together once more. I sat with Chiver on the ground in the shade in front of their house. Memène was standing behind him in their doorway, watching as the two kids lay in his lap. His boy was snacking on a small piece of boiled pumpkin as he maneuvered into a comfortable position, resting his head on one of Chiver's thighs. Memène's girl's right hand was playing with Chiver's bony kneecap, while she rested her head on his other thigh.

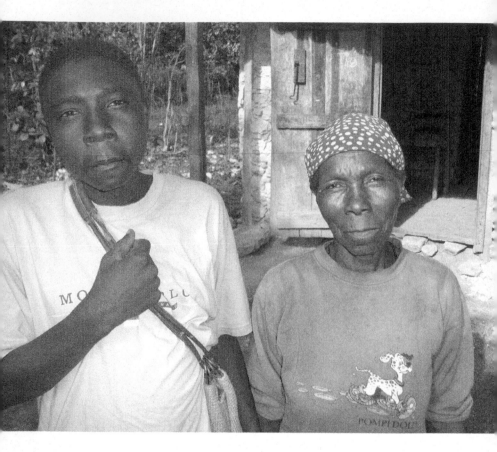

Jacquesonne and Manie

≥ 23 ≤

Jacquesonne's School

The first structure you see as you cross over the ridge into Mannwa is a church. It sits on a small hill to the left of the main path, above the mango tree that is also where the narrow, winding paths to Nan Joumou and Wòch Djèp meet the one that leads up from Viyèt. The church houses a community school that takes local kids through the third grade.

I hiked up several times in December, when I was still trying to convince a few more families to join the program. The first time I made the trip by myself, I found Jacquesonne standing in front of the school, taking in the scene as the school children played. It must have been recess. He's Manie's youngest son, a 16-year-old boy whom I met when I visited his mother''s house during the verification process.

I asked Jacquesonne to be my guide, knowing that I would have had a hard time finding the homes on my own. He agreed, so we spent most of the day walking around together.

He's a short, wiry boy with broad shoulders, but no extra meat on his bones. His pronounced overbite affects his speech and makes his smiles rare.

We spoke little as we walked, but at the end of the day, I paid him a little bit for his time. Then we went back down the dusty hill together. It was still early in the dry season. Harvest was over, and the fields were left with the traces of bean plants and dried stocks of corn and millet. The last bits of green were disappearing from the tall wild grass. The bleating of the goats and the lowing of the cattle signaled their late afternoon hunger.

We stood for a few minutes in front of the home where he and his mother lived, and I asked him what he had been doing up at the school. His bare feet and torn shorts told me that he wasn't attending. It was a steep, half-hour hike up from his mother's house to the school, so I didn't think he would just have wandered there. I wondered whether he had been sent on an errand of some sort.

"When I have nothing to do, I walk up to watch the kids." To watch them. He's never been to school himself. His mother has never been able to afford it.

When I got back to the office in Saut d'Eau, I told Gauthier the story. I said that I wanted to send Jacquesonne to school. He smiled. He couldn't even be bothered to say, "I told you so." It isn't his style. He had warned me when I joined his team that I'd find myself wanting to reach into my wallet once in a while. "I'm not going to stop you," he said, laughing as he leaned over his desk.

I was in Mannwa a few weeks later with Martinière. I let him know that I was looking for Jacquesonne. The rains wouldn't begin for another month or two, so there was no farm work for him to do. We found him hanging around in front of his mother's house, seated on the root of a tree, leaning back against the trunk. He had just returned from foraging for scraps of firewood, hoping that his mother would start a cooking fire once Martinière had finished with his visit.

Martinière and I spoke to Manie first. She seems really devoted to the boy, just as he seems devoted to her. She wants him in school, and hopes that the livestock that we gave her will enable her to send him next fall. Her other children are older. It's too late for them to start. But in Jacquesonne she has one last hope. We told her that she'd need to get ready to pay for school next year, but that we wanted to get Jacquesonne started right away and we were willing to pay for it.

When we were finished talking with her, we asked Jacquesonne whether he could take us to the school principal's home. We didn't tell him why. As we were speaking to Manie, he had kept a respectful distance. Rural kids are taught to disappear when adults are talking with one another. When we got to the principal's home, we asked him what we would need to do to get Jacquesonne into school right away, midway through the school year.

Jacquesonne's jaw dropped. As we negotiated and then paid the school fee for the year, Jacquesonne could only watch. We left the principal's *lakou* together. But once we got to the main path, we'd go our separate ways. Martinière and I were ready to head back down the hill toward our office. Jacquesonne would be turning back uphill to his mother's house. So we stood together in the middle of the path to talk before we separated. We needed to know whether he had shoes, socks, underwear, pants, and t-shirts that could be cleaned to look ok. He'd eventually need a uniform, but that would take some time. The principal was willing to let him come right away without a uniform, or "in civilian clothes" as they say in Haiti, but he'd need to look more or less decent anyway.

Jacquesonne had nothing but the torn shorts and t-shirt that he was wearing that day and had worn the day he served as my guide. No amount of cleaning would make them presentable. He'd need a whole new wardrobe. So Martinière and he made plans to meet at the Domon market and buy everything he'd need.

We said our goodbyes, and Martinière and I got ready to head down the hill. "*Lendi m pral lekòl,*" Jacquesonne said. "I'm going to school Monday." The matter-of-fact-ness of these words, their expression of a simple, unexpected realization, was as striking as the excitement submerged beneath them.

On Friday, Jacquesonne met Martinière in the market in Domon. It's easily a three- or four-hour hike each way to Manie's house, and Jacquesonne was now lame. He had stubbed his toe painfully on a tree root while walking barefoot around his mother's front yard just after we had seen him, ripping off a toenail. He was limping badly. But he made the walk and spent an hour in the market with Martinière.

He didn't know how to try on clothes. He was 16, and it was as if he'd never done it before. He needed sneakers, but when Martinière handed him a pair to try on, he put them on the wrong feet. He needed a couple of pairs of jeans, but chose the first pair his eyes fell upon, without looking to see whether they might be too big or two small.

He needed t-shirts and underwear and socks and a belt, and every purchase was a struggle. Jacquesonne would grab the first of everything he saw, as though worried that his shopping trip and, perhaps, the reason for it might turn out to be a dream. Martinière had to give lots of firm guidance. But they finally got their shopping done. Jacquesonne had even come with a handwritten list that the principal had given him of all the books he'd need. They bought those, too, and a book bag to carry it all in. All told, Martinière and I spent about $50. Martinière wished him luck, and watched him limp off toward home, his book bag slung across his shoulder and a black plastic bag full of his new clothes balanced on the top of his head.

So Jacquesonne is excited. We hope it lasts. He has a tough road ahead of him. He'll be sitting in first grade with kids less than half his age, kids who are now well ahead of him. And his speech impediment surely means he's in for some teasing. Limping to Domon showed a lot of determination of a certain kind, but the determination to face the small, daily difficulties and embarrassments that will follow is another matter. Especially when it means giving up money he could be earning in people's fields.

In a sense, his situation is emblematic of what our members face as they join our program. They suddenly find that they have access to resources and support that they could hardly have imagined. They have assets to manage, food to eat, and a well-trained advisor to guide them. But their daily struggle to change their lives has just begun.

PART IV:

BETTER LIVES

Pito w mize nan wout, ou pote bon komisyon.
(Better to take your time,
as long as you bring good news.)

Patrick and Jean Manie

≥ 24 ≤

Jean Manie and the Cabecita

Jean Manie was in her own home. Her little house belonged
to her. But her problems were a long way from solved. There
would not have been much point to her new freedom if she had
escaped from Moussa's house, where she and Patrick at least were
eating, only to go hungry.

Case managers have a simple means they use as a last resort
when they need extra support to help a member who's in an especially difficult situation. We have monthly meetings of our entire
staff, and they use those meetings to pass the hat. They reach into
their own pockets, and they ask their supervisors and colleagues to
do the same.

Case managers are not wealthy. Their salary is modest. And
many have spouses and children to support. Even those who are
single live with the Haitian reality that people who receive steady
paychecks – even small ones – will have friends and relatives who
depend on them. Alancia herself is a single mother with a boy, Josh,
just about Patrick's age. She wouldn't have a lot of money to spare.

But the team is large, and it's rare that a case manager won't be
able to collect anything. Alancia eventually collected about 2,000
gourds, or about $50, and planned to replace Jean Manie's pig.

Then she had second thoughts. She considered how much care
pigs require. She thought that Jean Manie would have a hard time
feeding one. Jean Manie didn't have money to buy feed, and she
didn't have land she could forage. Alancia also thought about Jean
Manie's savings and the money from the first pig. Between the mon-

ey she collected from the staff, the money from the meat that Alancia was eventually able to extract from Madan Moussa, and Jean Manie's savings, Alancia was able to help her buy a very young bull instead. Claude agreed to keep it for her until it was large enough that they'd be able to sell it and buy a female.

That was a plan, but it would not address Jean Manie's most urgent problem. Years of working in Moussa's fields had made her a capable farmer, but since she didn't have her own land, she wouldn't be able to feed herself and Patrick without buying food. She needed a steady income, something she could count on every day.

The fastest way for her to start earning one would be for her to go into small commerce, but there were difficulties to overcome. First, Jean Manie had rushed into her half-built home when only one of her two rooms had been completed. It was understandable. Idana tried to make her welcome, but Jean Manie couldn't help feeling as though she was in the way. Idana's house was small, and it was full even without Jean Manie and Patrick.

But Jean Manie's one room didn't have a door. She would not be able to start a business until she was living in a home that she could close up and lock. Otherwise, her merchandise could disappear any time she turned her back.

Second, Jean Manie was unaccustomed to dealing with money, and she had serious trouble with even simple calculations. The first time I asked her to add up a series of imagined purchases, her total was *"san katòz di goud,"* or *"one hundred fourteen ten gourds."* The words make no more sense in Creole than they do in English.

So Alancia pushed Jean Manie and Claude to get a door on the house. Claude bought a padlock for Jean Manie from a hardware merchant in Domon.

Alancia then decided to help Jean Manie establish a small commerce by proceeding along three lines. First, the two of them would choose a business that would be as simple as possible; second, she would have Jean Manie leave the largest regular transaction, the purchasing, in Claude's hands; and, third, she would have other

CLM members sit next to Jean Manie in the market, keeping an eye on her.

Jean Manie would start with only one product. She and Alancia chose kerosene. Jean Manie would give Claude the money to buy two gallons for her in Domon. It would be cheaper there. She would then sell it in small bottles in the local market in Feyobyen. She'd have very little calculating to do. The prices for kerosene are clear. There's nothing to negotiate. Jean Manie could refuse to accept large bills. And the other women would be with her.

The system worked.

Her income was very small, but steady, and she started getting used to business. And not just used to it. She liked it. She had been a field hand and a housekeeper all her life, and quickly discovered that she enjoyed the bustle of the market. She liked the camaraderie. She liked the gossip. She liked being part of a scene.

She soon began to feel that her kerosene wasn't selling well enough, so she decided to sell *kabesik* instead. *Kabesik* is low-grade rice, imported from the Dominican Republic, where it's used mainly as animal feed. It consists of partial grains that are discarded because they were crushed during the milling process. The Dominicans call it *"cabecita."* The Creole word comes from the Spanish. In central Haiti, *kabesik* is a staple for families who can't afford anything else.

Jean Manie would have Claude buy 600 gourds worth of *kabesik* on Fridays, at the market in Domon. That's about six large coffee cans of it. She could sell five of the coffee cans of it, small scoop by small scoop, for the same 600 gourds in one or two days in Feyobyen. She'd use the sixth can of it to feed herself and Patrick. Between that rice, and the various things she could take out of fields she would work in, she'd be able to keep the two of them fed. Patrick even began to put on some weight. Her success was wonderful even as small as it was, because the business was entirely her own plan.

That may not be the kind of progress we hope for, but eventually her livestock should help her increase her wealth. The goats should begin to multiply, and as soon as the bull has grown enough she'll exchange it for a cow that will be able to give her calves.

But her animals won't do very much in the short term. If her livestock and her commerce are all she has to work with, her progress will be very slow.

There is, however, another factor. Jean Manie is a young woman, and at various times over the years she's had suitors. Nothing much could come of the relationships while she was living with Moussa and his family. Men had to go through him. He would insist that they help her work in his fields, and his demands would eventually discourage them. Moussa had very little reason to want Jean Manie to marry eventually and move away.

Things changed when she moved into her own home. Shortly after she finished her house, a local farm laborer moved in with her, and things looked promising for a short while. He was working some at a nearby sugar mill, and would bring home logs of dark brown sugar called "*rapadou*," which are popular in rural areas of the Central Plateau. Jean Manie would sell the *rapadou* by the slice, and earn a nice addition to her income.

The relationship unraveled when Jean Manie got sick. She had learned from Alancia that she should go straight to the hospital. The doctor who saw her told her that she had a treatable infection and that she should refrain from sex during the couple of weeks she'd need to recover. When she got home and told her new partner the news, he got angry, claiming that it was just a story she was using to put him off, and he moved out. A couple of weeks later, he wanted to move back in, but Jean Manie said she wouldn't take him back.

That made him even angrier, and he said that he would have sex with her whether she was willing or not. Fortunately, Jean Manie told Alancia, who reported him to the police before anything could happen. Alancia also spoke to the guy, letting him know that she'd have him arrested for rape if he carried out his threat.

Not long after, a second man started showing interest in Jean Manie. This time, Jean Manie sent him to Claude. She chose to put Claude *in loco parentis*. Claude talked to the new boyfriend about his prospects and intentions, and he liked what he heard. He's a middle-aged widower with grown children. He showed no interest in having more kids, and was willing to help Jean Manie take care of Patrick. He had his own productive farmland, so he was able to contribute to the household. He initially wanted to have Jean Manie and Patrick move in with him, but Claude insisted that Jean Manie stay in her own home, and the guy eventually agreed.

But a few weeks into the relationship, they came to a bump in the road. The man hadn't yet brought a bed into their home, and Jean Manie was tired of sleeping on a straw mat on the ground. Even the previous boyfriend had brought a bed, though he had taken it with him when he and Jean Manie broke up. So she decided to throw the guy out.

When Jean Manie graduated in July 2012, her situation was still precarious. She had goats and a cow, but couldn't really manage them. Claude did it for her. Her income was small, just about enough for her to feed herself and her son, and wasn't likely to grow very much. She hadn't shown much evidence that she'd become more than marginally capable of business. Even with the intensive work she had done with Alancia, only the support of other women in the program had enabled her to keep her little business going. Her best chance appeared to depend on whether she could eventually establish a healthy relationship with a man who would help out. The hopeful part of this story is that Jean Manie seems willing and able to insist on what she feels she deserves from a man.

With the help of Claude and Alancia, Jean Manie escaped from Moussa and began a new life with Patrick in her own house. Talking about what would make her angriest about all the years she spent with Moussa, she wouldn't mention the physical or other abuse she suffered. She didn't talk about feeling hungry or exploited. She would say she had been a slave, but she never treated that as the most important thing.

She talked instead about Patrick, and about how little consideration he received. Moussa and his wife, she would say, showed no concern for the boy: "*Yo pat bezwen konnen, si yon ti gason bezwen manje, bezwen bwe.*" They didn't care even whether Patrick had anything to eat and drink.

Once, Jean Manie explained what she meant by talking about something that happened on a Sunday after church. Patrick was hungry, so he dug up a sweet potato in Moussa's field and boiled it. When Moussa saw, he told Patrick never to take anything from his garden again. Jean Manie said, "I was so angry. All the years that I'd planted and harvested those gardens, and prepared every bit of food the family ate, and Moussa couldn't let my boy eat a sweet potato."

Jean Manie is not and will not be alone. She has Claude. He gave her land to build a home on and much of the material she'd need to build it with. He took over managing her livestock, and helped her start her small commerce by doing her buying. He accepted the role of the father she didn't know when suitors came to her door. And Claude is determined not to fail. "I look forward to the day when people see Jean Manie's success and say, 'Look at what Claude did for her.'"

Jean Manie's life after she graduated was nothing like what it had previously been. She was not the same woman we met when we first visited Moussa's home. She herself decided to be one of the speakers at her graduation ceremony. In front of an audience of several hundred, she proclaimed that she was no longer a slave.

And the difference was more than just a change in attitude. She had built a modicum of wealth and a new way of life. She had friends, and in Claude she had something like family. But the difference was even more visible in Patrick. At Moussa's, he had been silent, scared, always looking at the ground. Once he and his mother were in their own home, he became a happy, healthy boy. He would charge up to me any time I appeared, and try to put my motorcycle helmet on his head. With the helmet on, he would run around with his arms outstretched, growling to imitate the sound of the motor. He was happiest of all any time I'd lift him up so he could sit on the motorcycle itself. At the end of the program, he was about eight, and was finally able to finish first grade. His mother dreams that he'll be able to go much farther than that. And maybe he will.

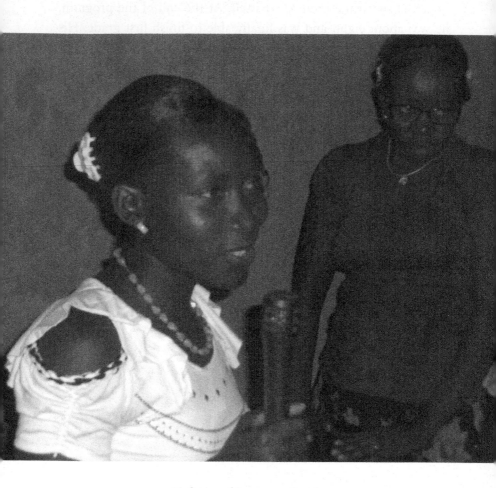

Ytelet speaking at graduation

⇒ 25 ⇐

Ytelet's Success

Once she was able to put her health scare behind her, Ytelet began to flourish. After a year, she and Dieulonet were living in a nice little house with her two kids. She had two goats, a pig, a small cow, and a range of barnyard fowl.

Her progress had little to do with anything tangible that we gave her, but it had a lot to do with how Martinière helped her learn to plan her life. We gave her goats and a pig, and after a year, her two goats were still just two goats, and her pig just a single pig. Neither had begun providing offspring. And yet she was making money and investing it.

Ytelet changed the way she farmed, and that was all it took to change her life. When she joined us, she had neither land of her own nor cash to invest. She worked her fields as a sharecropper, giving a third or even half of her harvest to the land's owner. When it came time to plant, she would borrow seeds or buy them on credit, paying two or three times their market price. There was no way for her to get ahead. Her poverty was much more than an unhappy circumstance. It was a part of a cycle.

Martinière's first objective was to help Ytelet accumulate some cash. He knew that once she had her own resources, she'd have a much better chance of holding on to her profits. So he encouraged her to be as economical as possible with the weekly food stipend she received during her first six months in the program, setting some of the money aside to build resources she could invest.

He didn't want her to overdo economy. Overzealous case managers can sometimes encourage families to save most of their stipend, even if they are experiencing hunger regularly. Ytelet would need most of the money to feed herself and her children. She and Martinière both knew how fragile her health could be. But she managed to accumulate some savings the way most of the women in our program do. She joined a *sòl*. When her turn came, Ytelet invested in beans.

She collected the pot during the harvest of pigeon peas. She bought about 20 *mamit* for 75 gourds each – a little less than $2 – and she held onto most of them until she was able to sell them for 125. A *mamit* is a heaping coffee can, a standard measure in Haiti.

Beans are one of the main cash crops in the mountains of the Central Plateau, and there are several harvests each year. At every harvest, Ytelet would buy as much as she could. She'd turn over some of the beans quickly, for a small profit, by simply carrying them down the mountain to sell in the markets in Chanbo and Feyobyen, where the prices are higher than in Zaboka. She would also hold onto some of what she bought as the price increased.

With some of the cash that she earned, she was able to rent a plot of land. In Tit Montay, they call it *"achte rekòt"* or "buying a harvest." Not only that, she had beans that she could plant. She wouldn't have to borrow them from wealthier neighbors. And so the yield would remain hers.

For the last crop before she joined our program, Ytelet had planted four *mamit* of borrowed beans. Her harvest was not great, but it was good, about 30 *mamit*. However, as a sharecropper she had to give half the harvest, 15 *mamit*, to the landowner. She paid back the four *mamit* of seed she had borrowed with 100% interest, or eight *mamit*. That left her with seven *mamit*.

Six months into her membership in CLM, she planted 12 *mamit* of beans that she purchased with cash up front on a plot she rented for 1,000 gourds. She put away 40 *mamit* of beans at harvest, even after using some of her harvest to pay the neighbors who had helped her to work the plot.

Between the sale of that harvest, and the profits from her ongoing bean business, she bought her cow. It should eventually provide calves, and will give her some milk that she can sell and drink, but it's not an investment that will repay her quickly.

It does, however, immediately change her status in the community. She no longer belongs among the poorest of the poor. And it also serves as an insurance policy, a big asset she can liquidate if she has a sudden need. A harvest later, she had purchased a horse as well, an investment that would be life-changing because it would mean she could bring more beans to market without even carrying them on her head. Her business would thus be able to grow.

And Ytelet made plans for her new income. She wants eventually to be able to send her children to school, and also to start buying farmland so she won't have to pay rent anymore. Her cow had grown enough by the time she was ready to graduate that she could have sold it to buy a small plot, but that's not what she wanted to do. When I asked her about that, she had an answer ready, *"Lè w gen yon bagay nan men w, ou retire l, ou mal pou antre l ankò."* That means if you let what you have pass out of your hands, you'll have a hard time replacing it. To Ytelet, it makes more sense to continue farming the land she rents until she has saved enough cash to buy land without selling off the assets she's accumulated so far. And who's to say that she's wrong?

Ytelet now manages her assets shrewdly. She keeps her goals in mind and has principles that she adheres to as she pursues them. She is nothing like the struggling, hungry young mother who entered the program. Martinière's ability to look beyond the resources we provide our members and help Ytelet see how she could farm more effectively made dramatic change possible.

But his fundamental contribution was something deeper. He knew from the start, from the depths of his heart, that Ytelet really mattered. He knew it when her family and neighbors had written her off. Her life didn't to them seem worth fighting for. His disinterested but ferocious commitment to getting her the care that she needed to survive taught both her and the people around her, more than words ever could have, that she was important enough to try to save.

Chimène and Guirlène, with Guirlène's children Guinya and Jovenson

PHOTO BY DARCY KEIFEL

≈ 26 ≈

Guirlène and Chimène

Guirlène was having a neighbor dig the hole for her latrine. The open pit made an attractive place to play for her boy, Jovenson.

One day, Jovenson was in the hole playing with his uncle Lukanchòn. Lukanchòn let a heavy iron pick fall in. The pick landed on Jovenson's foot, and pierced it all the way through. He was eight at the time, and Lukanchòn was a couple of years older. The boys had been playing in soft dirt, so the pick and both the boys were filthy. The dirt got right into the wound.

Guirlène didn't know what to do. This happened on a Friday morning. Her case manager, Nerlande, wouldn't be back in the neighborhood until Monday. She had no money to pay a motorcycle to bring herself and her boy to the emergency room. Though the care would be free thanks to Partners in Health, there would be transportation to pay for and food to buy if they had to stay overnight. She could have called Nerlande, but Guirlène had just joined the program, and was not yet used to thinking of her case manager as someone she could depend on.

So she was relieved when a neighbor said he would help. He rinsed the wound with strong, locally brewed rum and wrapped it with cotton wadding.

By Monday, when Nerlande and I went by, Jovenson was stuck in bed with a high fever and a badly swollen foot. We didn't waste many words. I picked him up and carried him up the short, steep path from Guirlène's house to the main road, huffing and puffing under the burden. I put him in front of me on my motorcycle, and Guirlène got on the back. Then we sped to the hospital in Mirebalais. Nerlande stayed in Pòsab to continue her day's worth of home visits.

Of course the foot was infected. And the wound had started to close over some of the cotton threads, so Jovenson went through agony as the Partners in Health nurses took care to pull out each dirty fiber. He screamed at them, begging them to leave him alone, as they carefully removed thread after thread. I stood half-hiding by the curtain that closed off his bed from the rest of the busy emergency room. Guirlène held her boy, crying as she forced him to let the nurses do their work. An X-ray showed that the pick had cut cleanly through flesh without damaging any of his bones. In that sense, he was lucky. The doctor who saw him gave him a course of children's Tylenol and amoxicillin, and sent him home.

But for all the misery the procedures caused him, Jovenson was quick to prove his resilience. I carried him back through the parking lot to my motorcycle, and tried to distract him by teaching him to honk the horn. He could reach it with his thumb without disturbing me as I drove him and his mother home. And he beeped at everything that moved all the way back to Pòsab.

ꕤ ꕤ ꕤ

When Guirlène first got together with Jovenson's father, Sonn, they moved to Belladère, east of Mirebalais on the Dominican border. Sonn drove a truck that would carry merchandise from Elias Piña, in the Dominican Republic, into Port au Prince. The work paid reasonably well, and he was able to support his wife and their young son.

Guirlène was pregnant with their daughter Guinya when Sonn made his last trip. The truck's brakes gave out as it was going down the dangerous mountain road that leads across Saut d'Eau to

Titayen. He had chosen that route, rather than the paved national highway, because he wanted to avoid the customs station that lies on the main road into the capital. Sonn never made it to a hospital.

After he died, Guirlène moved back to Pòsab, a small community near the market in Labasti, right on the main road from Port au Prince to Mirebalais. It was where her mother was living.

She wasn't on good terms with Chimène. Neither Chimène nor her father had accepted her relationship with Sonn. But she got on well with her stepfather, and he set up an *ajoupa* for her on a small corner of his land above the house he shared with Chimène. He covered it with the tin that Guirlène had taken off the roof of her home in Belladère.

Sonn had been the provider in their household. Guirlène's work had been to manage the money that he brought in. She hadn't ever earned a living herself. She didn't know how. So when he died, she wasn't sure what to do. She kept herself and her children fed by selling off the household goods that she had accumulated during her married life. Every time she needed cash, she sold something. One time a sheet, another a curtain, another a cast aluminum pot.

☡ ☡ ☡

I took Jovenson back to the hospital two days after the first trip to have his bandage changed, and he was already doing much better. Though he was sitting in a chair when I got to their *ajoupa*, unable to move around much on his still-painful foot, he was cheerful. He's a beautiful little boy, with large, dark eyes. His skin is light brown, so his family likes to call him "Blan." He shook my hand and smiled when I appeared, greeting me with a friendly, "*Bonjou, tonton.*" I carried him back up to the motorcycle, teasing him about how heavy he was. The big hospital had just opened, and they weren't yet set up to do non-emergency bandaging. So we went to the smaller clinic instead.

The rebandaging was painless. His nurse pretended to flirt as she was working on him. He is very sweet. Everyone who comes in contact with him falls in love. He seemed to enjoy her joke, and he certainly enjoyed the surprising painlessness of the procedure. He giggled when I warned him not to make Nerlande jealous with his new girlfriend.

When I returned to Pòsab another couple of days after that, he was playing. Though he still had a pronounced limp, he was happily seated on the saddle-shaped stem of a large palm frond. He had driven a short stick through the neck of the stem and was holding the stick's two ends like the handle bars of a motorcycle, revving the engine by growling and occasionally yelling "beep" to warn imaginary traffic to get out of his way.

The experience of his injury would have shaken any mother, but it was especially hard for Guirlène. Once she became a widow, Guirlène got used to referring to Jovenson as the man in her house. She is always raving about how loving and helpful he is. Not only does he refuse to complain when she can't feed him the way she'd like to, but he begs her not to borrow money or buy food on credit because he doesn't like to hear people speak roughly to her when she cannot pay. He would rather go hungry. Haitian children are generally raised to share. From their infancy, the adults around them will ask them for a little piece of any treat that comes their way, and by the time they are toddlers, sharing will become routine. But Blan is especially good about doing so. Nothing falls into his hands without his mother and his little sister getting some first.

A few days after my last visit, I got a call from Nerlande. She wanted me to see Guirlène and Chimène with her. She was worried. Their relationship was deteriorating, and that just made life harder for both. Guirlène still got on well enough with her stepfather, but the two women would argue and fight.

Chimène had problems enough of her own. She had young children she was struggling to feed. She also had an older daughter in Port au Prince who counted on her help.

Guirlène and Chimène would fight over everything and over nothing. Chimène wanted Guirlène to respect her authority. Guirlène resented the way her mother took advantage of her need to sell off her things. She had expected help when she had returned home a widow. Instead, she felt her mother cared about nothing but getting a good deal.

Nerlande was especially concerned because Guirlène was accusing Chimène of indifference to the damage Lukanchòn had inflicted on her boy. Guirlène was so angry that Chimène sent Lukanchòn to her daughter in Port au Prince. She was afraid of what Guirlène might do to him.

Nerlande led Guirlène and me into Chimène's small house. Guirlène wasn't happy about it. She didn't want to talk to her mother at all. But Nerlande insisted, and she relented. Nerlande started the conversation by talking about how hard it was for her to understand that a mother and her daughter would be unable to get along. But Guirlène quickly cut in. It had been days since her boy had been hurt, and Chimène had never once gone by Guirlène's home to ask about him, her own grandson. She hadn't sent either of her boys, either. "She doesn't care if Blan lives or dies."

"I don't care? How could I not care? Blan is my daughter's son. He's my very own child."

The two women were soon yelling at the same time. Each showed me where she had been wounded on occasions in the past when they had come to blows. Guirlène had a small scar near her neck, where Chimène had hit her with a belt. Chimène had one on her finger from a bite. Before long, Chimène was on her knees, with her hands lifted to heaven, swearing to God that she loved her daughter and her daughter's boy.

Nerlande and I had to admit that we weren't getting anywhere. Most of the anger was on Guirlène's side, but she had enough of it for both of them. So we asked them just to avoid each other. But we also got Guirlène to promise that she wouldn't harm Lukanchòn, her half-brother. We wanted to make sure it was safe for Chimène to bring him home. She claimed that it wouldn't have occurred to her to hurt him. She wasn't angry with Lukanchòn.

Even as we were following her drama, we also watched the progress the Guirlène was making. The weekly stipend began to do a lot for her and her kids. They ate more regularly, and Guirlène joined a *sòl* with 14 other women. When it was her turn to take the pot, Guirlène used it to address her biggest problem. She added its 1,500 gourds to the 500 she had left from the sale of her bed, the most valuable remnant of her life with Sonn, and put the 2,000-gourd total down as a first payment on a five-year lease on a small plot of land. The lease was 5,000 gourds, but the landowner liked Guirlène, and was willing to accept a partial payment. With her stepfather's help, she moved her *ajoupa* 50 yards downhill from where he had first built it. That got her out of her mother's yard, and made it possible for her to start to feel better about her life.

We were glad soon afterward when we saw that Guirlène had started a small commerce. It was an important step toward ensuring daily income. When she joined our program, she had asked us to give her goats and a pig. She and her boy took good care of her animals, but the livestock could not help her feed her children in the short term. She needed to earn at least a few gourds every day, and small commerce seemed the most likely way for her to do so. But we wondered where Guirlène had gotten the money to get started because we knew that the down payment she made on her lease had cleaned her out.

Her explanation surprised us. She told us that after she paid 100 gourds into her *sòl* each week, she would always take 25 of the remaining 200 gourds and give them to Jovenson. To an American accustomed to a culture in which even young children get an allowance, this might seem like an ordinary thing to do. But of the thousands of women who have been through our program, Guirlène is the only one we know of who has done anything like it.

And Jovenson decided to start his own little *sòl*. He wanted to save up money just like his mother had. He found neighbors, mostly other children, who were interested. A few adults joined, too. When it was Jovenson's turn to receive the 400-gourd pot, he gave it all to his mother and told her she could start a small commerce. She started selling cookies, crackers and hard candy from a basket at the side of the main road. Eventually she was able to add cash when her second turn came around to take the pot in her own *sòl*. That allowed her to diversify the range of products she would sell. She added peanut butter sandwiches and coffee that she would roast and grind herself. She would also occasionally fry dough or sweet potatoes. Things were moving forward.

We were discouraged a few months later to see that Guirlène's commerce had disappeared. She had used part of the capital to buy the lumber she needed to construct a more solid house on her land. Part of it had gone to pay school fees and buy textbooks for Jovenson. But a large chunk disappeared, probably ending up in the hands of a thief. Her six months of weekly stipends had passed, and now her income had returned to zero.

Within a couple of weeks, however, she was selling stuff by the side of the road once again. When we asked her where the capital had come from, she told us that she had organized another weekly *sòl*, this one for 100 gourds. We knew she had no income, so we asked her where her weekly contributions were coming from.

Guirlène said that she paid them from her commerce, and then explained. When organizing the *sòl*, she had told everyone who joined that they would have to let her collect the first pot. In a sense, she had arranged an interest-free loan from the group, and she immediately started a business that would allow her to pay it back.

Both Guirlène and Chimène continued to make progress. Chimène's livestock began to multiply. Her husband and their two boys worked hard to keep them healthy and growing, and so they prospered. Guirlène struggled with her livestock, but her small business was always there. It was sometimes larger and sometimes smaller, but it never disappeared entirely, so she, Jovenson, and Guinya managed rather well.

About nine months into the program, we held a training session in Niva, down the main highway towards Mirebalais from Pòsab. Nerlande was leading the session, and I went by to have a look. The territory we were covering was large, so we had organized the session at several sites simultaneously, and I had more than one place to visit.

I was surprised to see Guirlène and Chimène sitting together, chatting and laughing. That afternoon, Nerlande came by the office, and I asked her about it. She said that the women had become friends. She believed that a better life for Guirlène and her children would depend, in the long term, on healing the wound separating her from her mother. So Nerlande invested a lot of extra time over several months talking to both women about their conflict.

And her encouragement yielded results. Guirlène decided to go to her mother and make up. "We can't both be members of this program and not be friends," she explained. "I'm friendly with the other women. I have to be friendly with my mother, too." So they became close once more. When Guirlène would leave her business for a few minutes, Chimène would send Lukanchòn and his little brother Dinaydo to help Jovenson cover for her. The three boys had long been inseparable, despite their mothers' conflict. But as the wound separating the two women began to heal, the whole lot of them began to resemble one household in two homes.

They all seemed to be making great strides, but this is where the story becomes hard to write. As a manager, I am responsible for several hundred families at a time. I usually find myself focusing on the handful of families who are having the most trouble. The more Guirlène flourished, the less I saw of her. I continued to pass by occasionally, but usually because of foreign visitors. Guirlène was so good at articulating the progress she had made and the plans she had moving forward that I would frequently lead delegations to her home so she could speak to people who came to learn about our work.

One day, Nerlande mentioned to me that Guirlène was sick. She had been having stomachaches for days. She was feeling ill enough that she couldn't take care of her kids, so the three of them had moved into Chimène's home.

Nerlande convinced them that Guirlène should see a doctor. She and Chimène took Guirlène to the Partners in Health hospital in downtown Mirebalais. The doctors there said that they thought Guirlène had some sort of ovarian cyst. She was also terribly anemic. So they began to treat her for the anemia, figuring that they could address the cyst once she had built up her strength.

As weeks passed by, Guirlène would get better for a while, and then get sick again. I would go by and find her strong, working at developing her business or doing laundry or other chores, and then I'd go by again and find her bedridden. Nerlande and Chimène saw to it that she kept seeing the doctor whenever she was supposed to.

As the program got to the 15-month mark, we were pleased to see that Guirlène seemed to be regaining her strength. She attended the final training session we had for members in her area, and spoke thoughtfully about her plans for the future. She had decided that her business just wasn't taking off in Pòsab. She would wait for graduation, then sell her house and move back to Belladère with her kids. It was, she thought, an easier place to do business, because there are several large markets near the Dominican border.

It seemed like a good idea. The man who had leased her the plot in Pòsab was willing to take back the land and refund her the money for the last three years of the lease. Between that and the money from the house, she'd have enough to make a strong start.

Her relationship with Chimène had its ups and downs, just as her health did. Guirlène had left her own house by now, but she wasn't stable at Chimène's. At one point, she moved a few hundred yards down the main road from Pòsab toward Mirebalais, into an abandoned shack in her mother-in-law's *lakou*. She had moved out of Chimène's house in anger because a neighbor had told her that Chimène was jealous and had been telling other women that Guirlène was flirting with her stepfather.

But a few days later, I saw Jovenson hiking back up the road with a large sack packed full of clothes on his head. They were moving back in with Chimène. Nerlande had convinced her that she shouldn't be too quick to believe any rumor that came her way, and Chimène had denied ever having accused her. Guirlène's health was declining again, and her stepfather simply insisted that her place was with her mother and with him.

It lasted a couple of weeks, and once again Guirlène seemed to improve. But then she went to her mother-in-law's again. She explained that she was following an herbal treatment there.

As the day of graduation approached, Nerlande and the whole team became busier and busier with preparations. Graduation was scheduled for Tuesday, and on the Thursday before it, Nerlande called me to say that she had just heard from Chimène. Guirlène was dead. The funeral would be on Sunday.

Nerlande couldn't be there. Her uncle had passed away, so she had a family funeral to attend off in the northern part of Haiti. But I went, and a couple of case managers were there as well.

The funeral was held in the driveway of a half-constructed mortuary just uphill from Pòsab on the road to Port au Prince. The case managers and I stood on a pile of construction gravel. There were about two dozen chairs farther up the driveway, next to the bright white casket. I watched Jovenson as he sat next to Chimène in one of the first chairs, his head bowed, his feet not quite touching the ground. His grandmother had found matching white dress shirts, black slacks and black bowties for him and Lukanchòn. They listened in silence as the young people who led the services went through a series of prayers.

I could hear very little of what they were saying, and the larger crowd across the street must have had a much harder time. But they made their way through the prayers, asking God for who knows what.

When they turned the casket to carry it to the graveyard, Jovenson broke down in screams. A couple of adults picked him up and carried him home. The cemetery was farther up the road, and we walked along the highway with the casket in front of us, the few dozen people who had counted Guirlène as a friend.

Rural Haitian cemeteries are messy places. Above ground tombs crack and fall to ruin. Weeds are allowed to prosper for grazing livestock. I stood on a mound of hard dirt, looking down at the men who were pushing the casket into the simple, concrete tomb. Lukanchòn was up close, watching them, but when he saw me he ran up through the crowd. He grabbed me around the waist, hid his face in my shirt, and wept. I bent down to whisper in his ear, and asked him if he wanted to go home. He could only nod. So we turned away from the burial, and walked back to his mother's house hand-in-hand. We stopped a couple of times along the way, as he would pull himself close and rest his head on my hip so he could hide his face again.

I went back to see Chimène the next morning. She offered me coffee, and we sat and talked. I wanted her to come to the graduation the next day, but she said she didn't have the heart for it.

I pushed a little, though. I told her that it would be a way to honor the daughter she had lost, and she finally agreed. She said she would come because I asked her to.

On Tuesday morning I stood outside the community center where the graduation would be held, waiting to see whether Chimène would appear. I approached her as soon as I saw her, and thanked her for coming. Then I led her over to Gauthier, who wanted to share his sympathy.

Graduations are celebrations. Joyful, encouraging speeches alternate with songs. Graduates perform dances and skits. The day culminates with the distribution of certificates and a meal. At Chimène's graduation the case managers served beans and rice with chunks of beef in a thin tomato and onion sauce to over a thousand people, graduates and their guests.

For almost all of those attending, graduation brought the usual measure of happiness with it. Women and their families are proud of their achievement. Many invite wealthier-though-not-wealthy neighbors or friends to attend the ceremony as their godparents, and these come to the festivity with colorfully wrapped graduation gifts.

But for those of us thinking of Guirlène, the day's joy was deeply tainted. She had worked so hard and so well to make a first set of changes in her life, and had shown the good judgment and determination that further progress would require. She seemed to have reached the verge of what could turn into a far better future for her two beautiful kids. Guinya might not even remember her mother. Jovenson surely would. And so would his grandmother. And so will I.

Rose Marthe with Martinière on Graduation Day

⇒ 27 ⇐

Rose Marthe

The Chanbo market sits next to the Boucan Carré River at a spot where the river turns especially close to the county's small downtown. Women who come to market from Lower Boucan Carré ford the river, entering at the *palan*, the livestock market where cows, goats, pigs, and horses are sold. Others arrive along the road that stretches east to west from Domon, along the national highway, to Feyobyen and the footpath that leads up to Tit Montay. Still more funnel down along the numerous footpaths that lead from Chanbo into the hills that rise to its north. Two small roads fork uphill away from the river, toward the main road, and on market day they are clogged with saleswomen of all sorts.

Rows of women, blackened by dust from the charcoal they have laid out on torn sacks in front of their stools, squat under their battered, wide-brim straw hats, their only protection from the sun. Other merchants find places on the ground or on small stools behind neat arrangements of rice, yellow cornmeal, flour, and sugar. The open sacks of white and light brown sugar are magnets for flies, which the merchants chase away with occasional sweeps of their busy hands. Stacks of bouillon cubes sit next to piles of onions, scallions and garlic. Little bundles of cinnamon, clove and anise lay ready for shoppers planning sweet porridge or hot chocolate for their evening meal. Turning onto another one of the market's twisted lanes, you encounter folded blue jeans and plastic sandals and batteries and coffee mugs and school uniforms. Another turn

reveals baskets of pumpkins, mangoes, okra, sweet potatoes, or avocados, according to the season. Poorer merchants, with smaller
businesses, march around with their merchandise on their heads,
calling out prices, offering bargains on garlic or underwear or rat
poison or laundry soap or watercress or antibiotics.

Long after he had finished working with the women from Mannwa, Martinière still traveled to Chanbo almost every week to buy
livestock for the new families he was working with in northern
Mirebalais. Though his business was at the *palan*, he would wind
his way through the market once or twice just to see whether any of
his people were there, taking a few minutes to ask them how they
were doing.

It wasn't always easy to find them. They had no regular spot to
sell from. Rural markets are like department stores. Similar items
sell in the same spots. So, what each of them lugged down the hill
would determine where she set up shop. One week, Chrismène
might have a stack of homemade *kasav*, a flatbread made of grated
manioc roots from her own field. Maybe Omène would bring a
basket of spinach. Rose Marthe often brought beans, either from
her own harvest or purchased at the market in Zaboka.

Martinière would get big hugs and give back bigger ones, and
he'd exchange a few words: "How are you? How are the kids? How's
the livestock doing? Are things going well? Any news of the other
women from Mannwa?" The women might ask his advice about the
little problems that are a part of every life. But then they all would
return to their own work.

I'd get my news from Martinière. I had been assigned to a new
region, across the mountains to the north from Zaboka and Mannwa. I couldn't get to the Chanbo market often.

But Mannwa had become a special place for me over the course
of my first 20 months with the program. It started with frustration.
I had struggled so hard, but so unsuccessfully, to recruit families
in the region. Only about half of the women who qualified for

the program in Mannwa were willing to join it when we started. Though several asked to join later, after they had seen what other women had begun to achieve, there wasn't much we could do for them by the time they were ready for us.

The extra trips I made had given me a more detailed knowledge of the neighborhood than I had for any other part of Boucan Carré. I had been in all its little corners multiple times. I felt at ease there. I loved hiking around its narrow, winding footpaths, taking in the wide vistas and the rural quiet.

There, as everywhere throughout Haiti, people would yell, "*Blan*," as I passed. But in Mannwa, the word rang as a nickname they had given to a familiar presence. Friendly questions would follow it. How was I doing? What did I hear from my family? Why was I out walking under the hot midday sun?

The extra time I spent in the area also helped me build especially close relationships with the members there. I saw more of Elga's wives and Rose Marthe and Josamène than I saw of the rest of the women our team was working with. I had had enough time to discover the most comfortable way to sit in the thick, gnarled roots of the mango tree behind Chrismène's house. I had learned to like relaxing on a little chair in the shade in front of Rose Marthe's house, waiting while she ran off to collect her goats. She'd always insist that I see every one of them. I enjoyed the way her kids felt free to grab my bag and rummage through it looking for treats, and the way Josamène's boy Frann would jump on me as I approached, hoping that I'd turn him upside down and swing him around and that his father would send him climbing up into the tree to cut down a coconut for me.

And visiting Mannwa usually meant spending a long day with Martinière. There is something special about him. His tirelessness, his devotion to the job at hand, and his constant desire to chat through the questions on his mind make him a great person to hike, work and learn with.

In July 2012, we held a graduation ceremony in Difayi for wom-
en from Mannwa, Viyèt, Dimaren, and the neighborhoods above
Mòn Dega. There was singing and dancing and speeches. We presented certificates to all the members in the region who met our
simple graduation criteria. Their children were eating every day,
and they had at least two sources of income and a minimal level of
productive assets. They had a plan for the future and the confidence
to believe they could achieve their goals.

It was the first CLM graduation I was responsible for. Our
whole team was so focused on the goals the graduating women
had achieved that we hadn't initially faced the fact that we would
suddenly be seeing the families much more rarely.

After the ceremony, as I looked around the crowded church
lakou, I saw a group of women huddled closely around Martinière,
weeping and hugging a man who towered over them all. His own
eyes were tearing up as he took the time to say a long goodbye to
each one. I had assumed that I'd continue to see the women now
and again, but almost six months passed before I had a chance to
hike to Mannwa to see how they were doing. After a year and a half
of steady contact, six months felt like a long time.

January 1 is an important holiday in Haiti. It's not just New
Year's Day. It's also Independence Day. Families stay home and eat
pumpkin soup to celebrate the slaves' victory over the French in
1804. The celebration continues on January 2. Families that have
any means at all eat one of their biggest and best meals of the year.

So I decided to spend the day in Mannwa. It was a day off from
work, so I wouldn't be expected to be anywhere else. And I would
be able to find everyone I wanted to see. Josamène would be at
home, listening to Lwidòn's endless chatter. I'd get to see Rose
Marthe, and she'd make me see all her goats. Omène and Christmène, Elga's two wives, would be happy to see me. Manie would
greet me with her sweet, tired whisper, wanting me to listen to the
latest trouble Jacquesonne had gotten into and about his successes

farming in her fields. Jacquesonne himself would be satisfied if I simply noticed how tall he had grown.

I took my motorcycle to upper Viyèt. Since January is the dry season, the route from Kafou Jòj had none of the mud that can make it such a beast when there's been rain. The exposed rocks still make you thankful for whatever shock absorbers a dirt bike can offer, because you know it could be worse. But the thick ruts are empty of the water that fills them during the rainy season, and there's no layer of mud to make you skid.

I left my bike at the end of the path, and walked straight up the hill to the main ridge. That first hike is steep and nearly direct. And it's always hot because it faces directly south and is completely exposed to the sun.

When I got to the top of the ridge, I followed the trail westward through the high flatland that Edrès shares with other wealthier farmers. It's the area's richest farmland, though in January the fields are mostly empty. Nothing remains but a few withered stalks of corn or millet and the dried sticks that had carried the year's harvest of pigeon peas. I continued along the narrow stretch that separates Boukankola to the south from Lalyann and Wòch Djèp to the north. Then I cut down the long path that slants down into Wòch Djèp. I wanted to see Rose Marthe first.

When I got to the house, I found her and her little sister, Tinwa, working in the kitchen. The younger children were playing in the yard, one eye on their games, the other following the preparation of the holiday meal. Sepavre was off looking after the livestock. Rose Marthe rushed up to me, but the kids got there first. Her little boys grabbed my legs and then took my backpack. They started rifling through it to see what I might have brought for them.

Rose Marthe pretended to be angry with me. I hadn't told her that I was coming, so she had nothing she could offer. Not because there was nothing in the house. Her family wasn't hungry anymore. They were eating three times a day. That was one of the first things

she wanted me to know. In fact, she and Tinwa were almost finished preparing their holiday stew and there would be plenty to go
around. An extra mouth or two wouldn't make much of a difference. But the food had been cooked with meat, and Rose Marthe
knows that I am a vegetarian. The strange fact that I wouldn't eat
what seemed to them to be the most desirable part of a meal was
a topic of much discussion any time I ate together with members
of the program. To Haitians who couldn't afford to prepare meat,
who couldn't always afford to make any food at all, that kind of
choosiness seemed weird. Generally, they accepted it as one more
aspect of my foreignness, so Rose Marthe was resigned to the fact
that I wouldn't want to eat what was in her pot.

Two years had passed since I had first made the hike to Wòch
Djèp, forced at the time to do it twice within just a couple of weeks.
At the time of my first visit, Rose Marthe was nine months pregnant,
barely able to move. I sat on the packed dirt in front of her door as
we talked, and she sat on a bucket, leaning back against the door-
frame in her effort to balance the burden she was carrying in front
of her. I had come by to verify a case manager's recommendation
that she be invited to join our program, and the evidence was all
around me: the decaying shack, the hungry little children clinging
lifelessly to her, the lack of any signs of livestock. Then I returned
to Wòch Djèp to find out why she hadn't come to the training we
invited her to. The newborn crying as he lay with his mother on a
straw mat inside the shack told me all I needed to know.

As I looked at the chunky vegetable stew that she and Tinwa
were preparing for the holiday, I thought back to what she had said
at her graduation: "Before CLM, I had nothing to help me live with
my kids. I used to tear up my knees, crawling around rocks and
climbing trees, just to collect a few leaves I could boil in salt water
so they'd have something to eat. I'd be off looking for a day of work,
and while I was out the kids would go to our neighbors to beg a
little bit of salt to boil the leaves with. My neighbors would chase

them, 'Shoo! Get away from here, kids!' And when I got home, the same neighbors would put me to shame. They'd tell me that I should just stay home. But I'd say to myself, 'The hell with them.' I needed to do something to feed my children."

Most of the speakers at our graduation ceremonies are either members of our staff or local community leaders. Every once in a while, one of our donors comes and speaks as well. Everyone tries to give the women a final measure of advice: keep taking good care of your livestock, don't fritter away the capital your business is built on, look for advice wherever you can find it, use the memories of where you've been to motivate you to continue the struggle to move forward. Nothing they say is very eye opening. The speeches culminate with a long one from Gauthier, our program director, who offers a final word of encouragement.

Gauthier is a man who can have neither clients nor employees. He has only family. To become part of his world is immediately to become his sister, his brother, his child. Working for him means working alongside a man who wears his passionate commitment to the people he works for and the staff he works with prominently on his sleeve. And not just prominently, but also clearly. His commitment is unclouded, unambiguous, guided by an unswerving compass that always points reliably from his deep love for his country and for his fellow human beings toward a better future for one and all.

His standard graduation speech rings convincingly as a blessing from a father to his children, and the women sit rapt. He doesn't tell them anything they haven't heard before, but hearing it one final time from a man whom they like to call "*papa*" or even "*gran-papa*" is an important part of the day.

But it is not the most interesting part of the day. We always reserve some time for a few of the women to speak about their experience in the program. They talk about where they were when they started and the challenges they faced along the way. Though the

women are almost universally shy when they first meet us, many
of them want to speak at graduation. At her graduation in Zaboka,
Ytelet insisted on talking about the way Martinière stood up in the
middle of a public hospital, yelling at everyone he could find until
reluctant nurses gave her a bed. At hers in Chanbo, Jean Manie
wept as she screamed to the crowd that she had once been a slave,
but that she wasn't one anymore and she would never be one again.

In Difayi, we were in a noisy, cinder-block church. Its interior
walls had been covered with smoothed-over cement and painted a
creamy lime green. The red aluminum roof was absorbing the heat
of the midsummer sun and radiating it downward toward us. The
boisterous, tightly packed crowd only made the room even hotter.

Martinière introduced Rose Marthe by speaking of her courage
and determination. He spoke of her bout with cholera and how she
had pulled herself through. Rose Marthe stood timidly, her eyes on
the floor, as Martinière spoke.

But then she took center stage. With the microphone in her
right hand, she hiked her small brown leather handbag up onto
her shoulder with her left. "My life was miserable. Today, when I
think back on those times, I feel like now I'm really on a roll. I feel
so good now that I should sing you a song."

She talked about the first serious challenge that she faced on
her road out of poverty: her decision to enter the program at all. "I
had neighbors all around me telling me not to join," she explained.

It was especially bad when I appeared. None of her neighbors
were used to seeing foreigners, and they tried to play on her fears to
convince her to refuse to join. "They told me that Steve would steal
my children and that they'd have me arrested right along with him.
But I thought, 'To hell with them.' I figured I had nothing to lose."

The same people who had been complaining about the way she
would leave her children to beg for a little salt were advising her to
forego the chance to change her life. It made no sense to her.

Her graduation speech was liberally peppered with a refrain:
"*Zafè y.*" Literally, that means "their business" or "their stuff." But in

the context it is just like saying "the hell with them." Rose Marthe had been getting lots of advice from people who had always been reluctant to help her, and she wasn't having any of it.

As Rose Marthe and I chatted on that day in early January, I thought of her speech and I looked around her yard. The children would be returning to school in a few days, and their clean uniforms were flapping in the breeze, drying on a line behind the house. The hike from Wòch Djèp to the school in Mannwa is long, but the kids were excited to go every day, and Rose Marthe was glad to be able to send them. Before she joined our program, she had never had the money to do so. The kids were finally healthy and well fed.

I didn't stay with Rose Marthe very long. It would be a long day, and I had more people I wanted to see. I'd hike down into Lalyann to see Magalie and then Elga and his wives, Omène and Christmène. Then I'd have the steep walk straight back up the north side of the hill to the top of the Mannwa ridge again, where I'd see Marie Paul, Manie, and Sorène.

Our program lasts for 18 months, or 21 if you count the time it takes to select the families who will participate in it. In a sense, it's work that can appear to have a beginning, a middle and an end. You choose a family, help the woman who leads it start a couple of small businesses, and coach her as she makes her way toward graduation. We have a method that addresses extreme poverty, and we have proven that the method almost always works. Over 95% of our families succeed. The most important lesson that our program has taught us so far is that extremely poor women – women like Rose Marthe and Ytelèt – can improve their lives if they are given a reasonable chance to do so. That lesson directly implies a corollary: Extremely poor families suffer the deprivations of their poverty because those of us who could give them that chance do not decide to help. Extreme poverty exists because we do not choose to eliminate it.

But the work doesn't ever really end. For someone like Rose Marthe, the challenges she faces to raise healthy, happy children don't go away after 18 months or 21 months or ever. Her last words at graduation were, "I used to go to market without anything decent to wear. Now I'm looking good." And she did a little spin so the audience – mainly her fellow graduates and their guests – could appreciate her full ensemble. Her bright yellow polyester blouse contrasted sharply with her dark, dark skin. The little ruffles around its shoulders got in the way as she slid the handle of purse from the crook in her bent elbow up her arm. She gave her shoulder a little flick to get the handbag all the way up over the bunched fabric to where it could hang down comfortably as she spoke.

Martinière had a protective arm across her shoulders as he introduced her and handed her the microphone, but he slid away, off to the side, as she began to speak. This was no longer a woman who needed his support. Rose Marthe still has to hike to the market several times each week to buy or sell as she struggles to further build her livelihood. But she faces those challenges with a new set of tools at her disposal. Her graduation was, even more than the many academic graduations I've been part of, a commencement rather than an end.

S and Gauthier

PHOTO BY PEG FOURRE

AFTERWORD
and
ACKNOWLEDGMENTS

I will always be grateful to David Diggs, of Beyond Borders, and John Engle, of Haiti Partners, for introducing me to Haiti. Their initial invitation and the supportive collegiality they showed me as I began to learn about the country were critical to my getting off on the right foot as I started to find my way.

Work on the writings that led to this book began in 2005, almost ten years after I first started visiting the country. I was moving to Haiti, and wanted a way to share something of my experience with students at Shimer College, my home institution, and with friends and family who might be interested. So I started to write short essays and post them online. I would produce something every week or two.

I knew nothing about writing things online, and I still know very little. But my ignorance has never been a barrier. Kendra Little did – and still does – whatever is necessary. Without her support, this project never would have gotten off the ground.

For several years, I continued to add short posts to the website Kendra had created for me. There are now quite a lot of them. But I never thought of doing more with them. The two to three pages I would write every couple of weeks gave me a chance to think about and share pieces of my experience that I found striking. That was all I was looking for. Nothing about the pieces themselves or about my experience in Haiti drew me to want to organize them into anything larger. They were scattered, hardly related. And that didn't feel like a problem to me. One week I'd write about something that happened at a meeting or a class. Another week I'd write about the challenges I faced getting around in Port au Prince or elsewhere in Haiti. And then I'd write about one of my neighbors or about the way that Haitians use different words to speak to different animals, as though Cattle-Creole and Chicken-Creole were distinct languages.

I certainly didn't want to write a book about Haiti. Many people much more qualified than I am had written books about the country already: journalists, historians, anthropologists, sociologists, and others. Nor did I want to write a travelogue, trying to astonish or entertain readers with tales from a part of the world that I sometimes felt to be strange. Writing about my experiences was a way to reflect on things that happened to catch my attention and share those reflections with my friends.

Everything changed as I began working for Fonkoze's CLM team. After having jumped around from place to place for five years, I finally began a single extended experience. I was still writing every week or two about whatever happened to occur to me, but my newer essays related to aspects of the same work or about the people it introduced me to. As the pieces continued to accumulate, I began to wonder whether they could somehow be organized into something larger. I just didn't know how to start.

At that point, two people intervened to make writing a book seem possible. I met Margaret Dulaney on one of her trips to Haiti. Her husband was then part of Fonkoze's American board. She was an experienced and successful author, and her strong encouragement and support was critical as I began to look at hundreds of pages of blog posts, trying to figure out whether I could stitch them together.

Through Margaret's connections I then met Nina Ryan, the editor whose firm, friendly and shrewd guidance taught me what I would have to do to transform my collection of little pieces into something like a whole. She became much more than an editor.

She became a teacher, coaching me through a process I had never even thought about. Though all the faults in this book belong to me and to me alone, anything that might be good in it owes at least something to Margaret's support and Nina's guidance.

As I developed the book, I decided to keep background information, whether about Haiti's history, its culture, or my personal life in Haiti, to a minimum. I wanted the book's focus, as much as possible, to remain on the work itself and on the women it touched.

Once I had a workable draft, I began to try to figure out how to get it into print. At that point, the book was adopted by two champions, Matt Balitsaris and Jeff Wright. Their knowledge of the publishing process and their willingness to provide the advice and resources publication would require have been essential as the book was traversing the final steps toward publication.

As for the book itself, it remains only to thank Cheri Parsons, who volunteered to make the maps we all felt that the book needed, and Dr. Paul Farmer, who very generously agreed to write a foreword. Mary C. Lewis provided critical advice toward a final shaping of the manuscript and Annette Leach took it through the last steps toward publication.

The work that I've undertaken to describe has depended on many people. I want especially to thank Erik Badger, whose counsel and friendship has been critical to my experience in Haiti – to my life, in fact – since he first joined me there in 1999.

The Fonkoze family of institutions, with its mission to fight exclusion from the Haitian economy, came to feel that it needed a special program to address extreme poverty and was willing to make me part of the team to bring it to scale. Staff from all three of its institutions, led by Carine Roenen Laroche, Leigh Carter and Matt Brown have supported every aspect of my experience in the field as part of Fonkoze and, more specifically, as part of CLM.

I would never have become part of that team at all without Anne Hastings, the former executive director of Fonkoze and the person most responsible for the CLM program's existence. I love and admire her more than she can ever know.

Many institutions have supported the work of CLM. We originally learned the program from BRAC, and then sought and received BRAC's help again when we were ready to make our program grow. Support from CGAP, Irish Aid and Concern Worldwide made the program's pilot possible. Once we demonstrated that the approach could succeed, a range of large and small partners joined the fight to eliminate extreme poverty in Haiti: the Haiti Timoun Foundation, the MasterCard Foundation, Fondation Kanpe, the Vista Hermosa Foundation, the Pathy Family Foundation, the Vincentian Family, the W. K. Kellogg Foundation, Artists for Haiti, the Caris Foundation, Texas Christian University, the Digicel Foundation, Haiti's Secretary of State for the Integration of Persons with Disabilities, the Riverside Presbyterian Church in Jacksonville, Florida, Schlegel Villages, the Swiss Agency for Development Cooperation, and numerous individual donors.

I am more grateful than I can say to the CLM team: the families it is our privilege to serve; the case managers who do the lion's share of the work; the drivers, administrators, and housekeepers who make the work possible; and my colleagues in management, especially Bethony, Hébert and Wilson, who have been my partners and my teachers in every aspect of this endeavor.

But one person deserves my very particular thanks: Gauthier Dieudonné, the director of the CLM program. Without the patient good humor and wisdom he has shown as my supervisor and the brotherly care he has shown for my well-being, the part I have played in the struggle over these past years would have been impossible.

ABOUT THE AUTHOR

Steven Werlin has been a faculty member at Shimer College, in Chicago, since 1996. He taught widely through the curriculum and served as Dean of the College from 2001 through 2004. In 1996, Steven began traveling to Haiti, where he was invited to observe literacy classes and talk with the people organizing them about ways to involve students in classroom discussions.

Living in Haiti since January 2005, Steven divided his time between a room in a house in Kaglo, a village in the mountains above Port au Prince, and three to four other residences. He taught classes for high school students, literacy center participants, primary school teachers, and groups as different as teenage boys from Port au Prince's largest slum and women from a network of rape victims.

Steven started working with Fonkoze as an advisor to its literacy and education department in early 2005 and continued to help with various projects for its communications, grant writing and education teams until March 2009, when he became the manager of its branch in the southeastern town of Marigot. Since 2010, Steven has been working for *Chemen Lavi Miyò*, or CLM, Fonkoze's program for the extreme poor. He began as a regional director and is now the communications and learning officer.

Steven keeps a blog about his experiences in Haiti at ***apprenticeshipineducation.com/blog***. When he's not in the field, he likes to sit on his front porch with his dog Lilly, drinking coffee and reading novels.